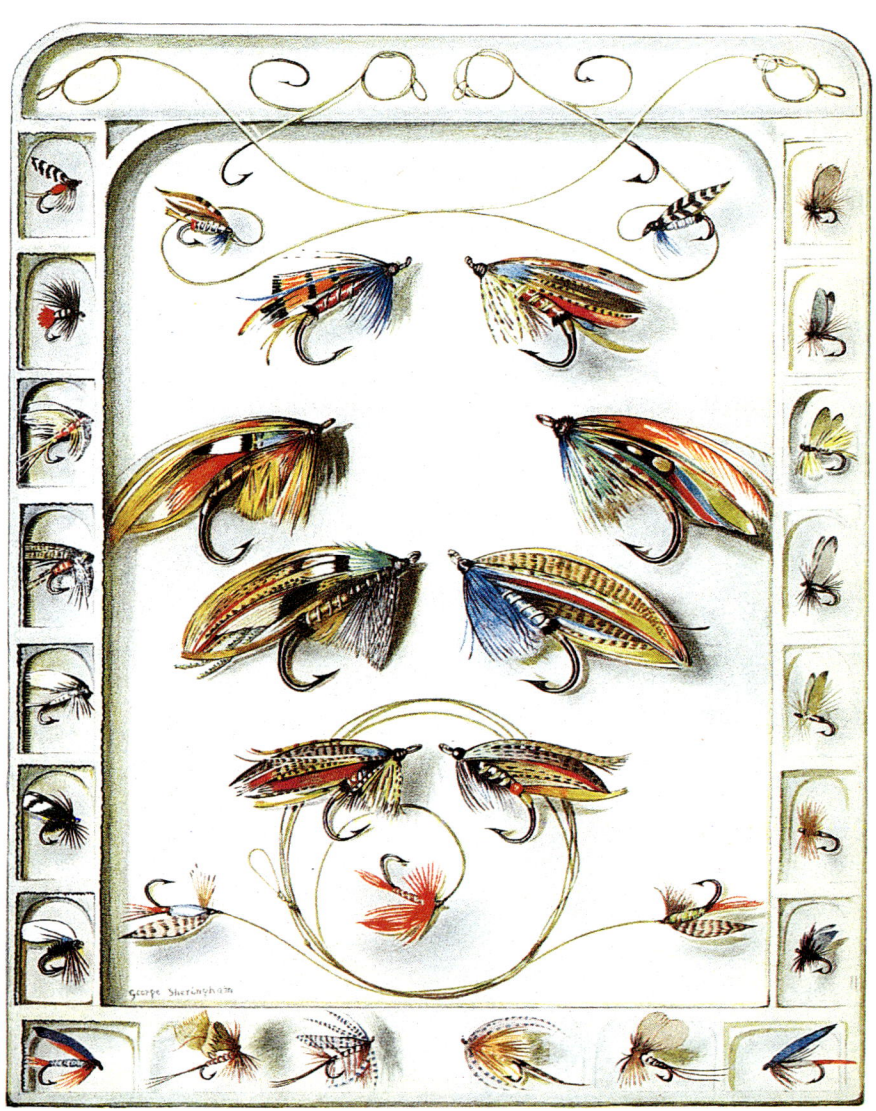

George Sheringham

THE BOOK OF
THE FLY-ROD

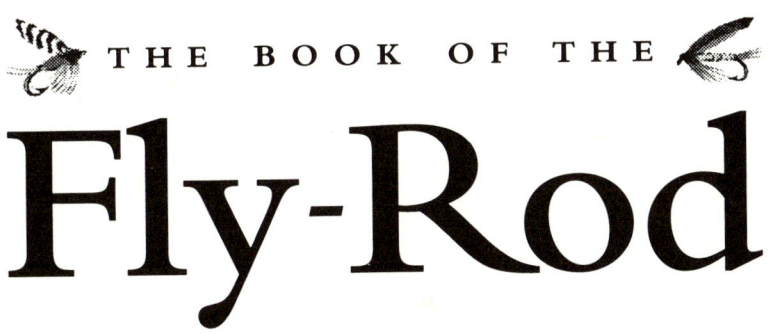

THE BOOK OF THE

Fly-Rod

edited by

HUGH SHERINGHAM & JOHN C. MOORE

illustrated by

GEORGE SHERINGHAM

THE DERRYDALE PRESS

LANHAM AND NEW YORK

THE DERRYDALE PRESS

Published in the United States of America
by The Derrydale Press
4720 Boston Way, Lanham, Maryland 20706

Distributed by NATIONAL BOOK NETWORK, INC.

Original Derrydale printing 1993
First paperback printing with french folds 1999

EDITOR'S NOTE

IN May, 1930, Hugh Sheringham asked me to help him with the editing of this book. His death in December left me with the sad job of finishing it alone.

The task has not been an easy one. I have been constantly wishing to ask his advice upon difficult questions, as I used to do. Now it is finished I hope that the final book is more or less as he would have done it.

A few words of explanation are necessary. He planned the book in such a way that it should treat the fly-rod in its widest possible aspect; so that the reader will here find it dealt with diversely as a magic wand which opens up a new world when we flick it, as an ambassador between nations, as the handmaiden of philosophy, the arts, and the sciences, and as a friendly companion wherever the angler wanders, be it east across Europe to Russia or west to Canada, Newfoundland, and the United States.

There are two omissions which need apology or excuse.

Australasia, which now provides what is probably the finest fishing in the world, is not represented at all. An apologetic editor can only explain that the contribution which should have told the history of these fisheries unaccountably failed to arrive. He tenders his humble regrets to a great continent.

The other omission is deliberate. Where, the reader may ask, is the Herefordshire Wye? Where are the great salmon rivers of Scotland?

The answer is that when a river becomes worth many thousand pounds a mile, that river ceases to concern the majority of anglers at all. It is fit only for a museum. It is, in fact, something of a joke.

Hugh Sheringham had little sympathy with the plutocrat who (his own words) " bestrides our streams like a Colossus." He liked to think of the fly-rod as something which all men equally could enjoy.

It was chiefly the humbler angler whom he loved and by whom he was loved in return. They wrote to him in thousands, and received and treasured personal replies in his familiar green ink. However overworked he was, he could always find time to tell the unemployed and hungry person how to catch chub for food —and who in all the world knew more about chub-catching than he? He was always willing to help local angling societies with support and advice; his house was a sort of village committee room, and the study where he worked all day would be turned suddenly into the meeting-place of an angling association or a boxing-club. Bits of the next week's *Field* would be hurriedly heaped together on his desk, and Hugh Sheringham would turn from them to be a genial and clever chairman, so that the meeting long outlasted its original purpose and became a memorable social occasion.

It is thus that H. T. S. should be remembered. He always preferred that a river should be bought by a large angling club than by a single millionaire or a syndicate of plutocrats. And so, although I make excuse, I make no apology that the very expensive salmon rivers do not come within the scope of this book. We have proved that the fly-rod is one of life's better things; we must therefore be all the more careful not to become superior about it.

That is all the explanation which is necessary, except, perhaps, that the final chapter, *De Minimis*, is the one which H. T. S. had intended to write himself. He could not do so, and with much diffidence I deputise.

I have now to thank several people. All the contributors have been kind and helpful and patient with me at a difficult time; my grateful thanks are particularly due to Mr. William Radcliffe, Mr. Ferris Greenslet, Mr. Harry Plunket Greene, and Mr. George Sheringham, each of whom has given me special assistance in various ways.

The latter has been the most obliging of artists. At the last minute I have said, autocratically, "Draw me a fish," "Draw me a weir," "Draw me a bloke fishing," and bloke and weir and fish have been duly forthcoming. Even when I sent him a roach which reached him in an advanced state of decay, he still made a beautiful picture of it.

This book is the result of his only collaboration with his brother, after they had each worked for many years in widely different spheres.

I have to acknowledge the kindness and courtesy of Messrs. Farlow, who lent the trout flies which were used for the drawings; and of Mr. A. Severn, of the Bibury Fish Farm, who was good enough to provide a fine specimen of a trout at the request of a worried Editor whose desperate efforts with the fly-rod, during two hot days, had proved of no avail.

Finally, let me say that I feel, in this book, very much like an understudy appearing for his principal; my great wish is that it would have pleased H. T. S., who was my very good friend.

J. C. M.

Guy C. Pollock

A MEMORY OF
HUGH SHERINGHAM

HUGH TEMPEST SHERINGHAM, whose work on this volume was cut short by death, was always known to a large number of his friends as H. T. S. And that, I think, is one of those trivial but significant pieces of evidence which inspire the accuracy of judgment. In this kind of initialled appellation there seems to me a blend of affection and regard which translates precisely the impression which Sheringham made on those who came closely in contact with him. He had great capacities for intimate friendship; so have a host of men. He was, as the old-fashioned phrase goes, "a scholar and a gentleman"; so are a very large number of unimportant people. He was highly skilled with a pen and most destructive with a fishing-rod; that is not an unusual combination of talents. But the secret something which made H. T. S. different was a gorgeously comprehensive sympathy.

I think that in later years, when, by force of circumstance, I saw comparatively little of him, this kind of brotherliness enlarged itself so much as to tinge all his views of life and men and things. But altered convictions were in him a part of that genuinely Christian spirit of trustful affection, toleration, and understanding which has a magnetic attraction.

However, in any sort of a Foreword to a volume on Angling, it is much more proper that I should try for a little to recapture the character of Sheringham when he was about the business of angling. Nor is this very difficult, because it was angling which first drew Sheringham and myself together more than twenty years ago. Of course, I know very little now of the unfathomable mysteries of fly-fishing. I knew less then. Ever since I first took a fly-rod in my hands during my summer holidays, at the age of eleven, I had fished industriously, and always for trout. I had undergone one curious experience with the dry fly when Andrew Lang–one of my father's intimate friends–had given me a day in June on some club water, on one of the then less polluted streams in Hertfordshire which he called "a muddy ditch." I had gone to Mr. Farlow, bought four winged may-flies, an oil bottle and a tin of grease, had taken the train to Ware and a "fly" to the keeper's cottage, had been completely bewildered by the attempt to practise a strange art until the keeper picked me up and began to instruct me, and had finished by catching a 2-pound trout and falling through a rotten fence on which I was leaning into 8 feet of muddy water, before I had put behind me this solitary exception to a career of wet-fly efforts on the streams chiefly of Dartmoor and Wales.

Anyhow, this interlude had taught me little enough when Sheringham's first book on angling came into my hands for review. And a week or so after I had written about it, I met Sheringham at some fly-casting tournament. Not because he cared excessively for the praise which I had given to his book, nor because I had an exaggerated reverence for his skill with the rod, but by one of those accidents which make so much difference to our lives, we then and there began a friendship which was never broken, and which, until the Great War fell upon us, brought us continually into each other's company, either in collaboration in unacted (and, I think, unactable) dramas or on banks of rivers.

His first concern was to teach me how to fish, and the charm of the man was proved by the fact that he did it quite rapidly and quite effectively, without ever letting me realise that what I had mistaken for experience and skill were ignorance and bungling, without ever wounding my deplorable self-esteem or losing his own temper. Once he did lose his temper with me and pretty thoroughly. But I was so conscious of crime that I was unable to lose mine in return.

We were staying and fishing with William Caine in a house he had some 5 or 6 miles from Salisbury and, being unable to find any feeding fish myself, I had wandered along to see what H. T. S. was doing on a small carrier which he had determined to explore. I found him crouched on the grass at the bottom of a little run, and by the motions of his hand I was given to understand his extreme dissatisfaction with my arrival. However, I crept along and crouched by his side, when I saw that he had in front of him an enormous and beautifully shaped trout of some 3 pounds, cruising up and down on the edge of the run and occasionally sucking down a fly. At the right moment, out went Sheringham's olive, with a flick which never carried the shadow of his rod or his arm across the water; up came the trout; Sheringham struck quite hard and jumped to his feet, holding the fish violently from a rush upstream which would have carried him to impossible places. We were all very excited, he and I and the trout, and, just as he had turned the head of the fish so that I saw its full size for the first time, I exclaimed "My God!", knocked against his arm, and decreed the escape of the trout.

I did not know, until I thought about it quietly that night, the full force or extent of the vocabulary of this gentle Christian man. And not even a 2-pounder, which he slew half an hour afterwards in the same run, by his lone and unhampered efforts, not the wit of William Caine, not the aggrieved silence of myself, nor even the fact that I had caught no trout at all, could drive the frown from his

[viii]

face that night. Perhaps he was remembering some of the terrible words which he used in addressing me and was ashamed. But I don't think he was!

Thus even one of the most amiable of men could lose his temper. And–another sign of human fallibility–even the Mentor of many of us could make a mistake about a fish. We were all, which is to say almost a gang of us who had interests of angling and literature in common, staying in one of the golden years and in a bitterly cold spring time at a little hotel in Wales, fishing for trout, which very often scarcely exceeded the size limit of what came to be known as "breakfast fish." Then, one Sunday afternoon, during his dignified walks abroad, H. T. S. discovered a monstrous trout, probably 2 pounds in weight, in a small side stream which fed the mill. He revealed the secret to me and later to the others, and reserved to himself the first attack, which was to be made on Monday morning with the dry fly. So we went along and, from a respectful distance, watched the attack. It failed utterly. And we told Sheringham so frankly and so volubly that he was incompetent, that he went away to fish elsewhere a little haughtily. Then we sat in a committee on his great trout and, at last, it was chased up from some weed beds below into the vision of three of us, who perceived quite clearly that it was nothing but a logger-headed chub. That joke lasted the whole party for the rest of the week.

And again, I remember going to Blagdon with H. T. S. and being particularly warned by him, on setting out for the first day's fishing, that if one were to lay hold of a really big one and find that no powers of rod or boatman could restrain him from going under the keel of the boat, then the thing to do was to plunge the rod point deep into the water, steer it round the bow or stern, and so avoid disaster. I took respectful note of the advice, wondering whether my presence of mind would equal the occasion if it occurred. Shortly afterwards, H. T. S. did battle with a real big one, not less, I should say, than 4 pounds and not more than 6 pounds. And, of course, what was inevitable happened. Towards the middle of the fight the fish gathered fresh force when he was quite close to the boat, made a dash underneath it, frayed the gut against the keel, and was gone. I think that Donald Carr wept. As for Sheringham and myself, we were silent until, very foolishly, I said to him, "But why didn't you plunge the rod point deep into the water?" It says much for his forbearance that he did not throw me into the lake–unless the reason was that he couldn't get at me. But he was seldom defeated for long, and, two days afterwards, when we had been fishing from the bank, he came back to our lodgings for a late supper with a fish of $5\frac{1}{4}$ pounds, which was, and is, the biggest trout that I have seen caught fairly and squarely with a fly. My own 3-pounder–reputed–with which I had been so ridiculously pleased, shrank at once to the size of a stickleback.

Such are the kind of incidents, joyous, irresponsible and, as young people said yesterday, "youth engendering," which come into my mind when I think,

B

as I often do, of Hugh Sheringham. Wonderful doses of conversation when spring fever had us in its grip, communal visits to tackle shops, and long days–so long as he could get a cup of tea at the right time, H. T. S. counted the hours of a day's honest fishing much as Stewart did–of intermittent companionship in Hampshire and in Wales. I always felt that in his heart of hearts he preferred the water meadows to the moorlands and the dry fly to the wet, whereas *my* secret heart was with the rough water swirling brown and eager round one's waders, with the $\frac{1}{4}$-pounder lying under the overhanging bushes of the opposite bank, and with the long trek home across the moor, with the occasional cock-grouse crowing angrily as he was disturbed and the curlew crying and whistling through the snow showers, towards the purple of the distant hill. But his methods were just as effective on one water as on another.

I do not honestly believe that if you were to have watched Sheringham using a rod you would have said that it was a pretty sight. I know many other anglers, men and women, whose handling of a rod is much more graceful. But if you stood by his side and watched, not the angler, but the line which he threw, then you saw the perfect grace which achieves the best result. He would tolerate no silly nonsense about making the fly light like thistledown on the water. He would rather slam the line down so that, in effect, the fly, that was gradually carried onward to the full extent of the gut cast, did light like thistledown. He had unorthodox views about giving a fish the butt of the rod and often preferred to kill him with a horizontal rod. And he had little mercy once the hook was driven in. To hustle the fish downstream, hold him hard, drown him and bewilder him, till he was drawn over the waiting net–those, I think, were his tactics, once the strategy had induced the fish to rise at him. But, of course, as is the case with so many other intelligent minds which devote a large part of their energies to the consideration of the sport of fishing, much of the heterodoxy which Sheringham imagined twenty-five years ago is orthodoxy today.

Short rods, light rods, heavy lines, and the controlled exercise of muscular force; dry flies for wet streams and lake fishing: the more angling remains the same in its appeal, the more it changes in its ritual. He had, of course, a multitude of rods and the tyranny of paraphernalia by which all honest anglers are oppressed. But he was used from time to time to lighten his burden by giving me a rod or a fly-box or a patent contraption of one sort or another. And when I had said to him, "What's wrong with the rod?" and he had said, "You always ask silly questions," we used to go away and make experiments with each other's rods in the continual search for the elusive secret of balance and handiness and strength. Sometimes, in this way, one of us would improve a rod which the other had lost patience with; at other times we ruined it. But, whereas I merely fumbled like the ordinary person who has a great interest in rods, Sheringham knew what he was doing; for his knowledge of this art which he practised,

[x]

whether of its literary history or its first editions, of its principles or of its weapons, was thorough. Thus he wrote about it year after year with an authority which continuously increased, with a charm and wit and humour which never failed.

There will always be new writers on angling, and they will always be good, since it is almost beyond the power of anyone who wishes to write about it at all to write badly about this sport, which is more properly called a vocation. But the outstanding names still slip through one's mind–Walton, Stewart, Edward Grey, Halford, Dewar, Earl Hodgson, and many others. And the name of H. T. Sheringham is secure in that company. He will always be a Triton among the Tritons.

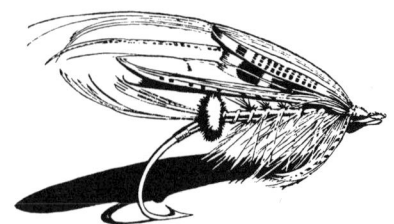

THE CONTENTS

THE ILLUSTRATIONS

PLATES IN COLOUR-COLLOTYPE

PLATES IN BLACK AND WHITE

by

Henry Van Dyke

DE MAXIMIS

THE editor of this *Book of the Fly-Rod* has asked me to write a chapter for which he has furnished the title. Generous, but embarrassing!

What *are* the greatest things about the fly-rod? Who knows? Opinions differ according to tastes. Divergent views are put forth with ardour, and sometimes with acrimony, as any reader of *The Field* or *The Fishing Gazette* may observe. Piscatorial controversy is not quite as fierce as theological; but it has a certain tempered sharpness of its own.

Shall I be entangled in the fray by writing this innocent chapter? Swiftly wounded by a dry fly from the rod of Hewitt or subtly pierced by a wet fly from the rod of Skues? Stoutly prodded in the ribs by a steel-centred rod or slyly caught around the neck by a limber greenheart? Heaven forbid! I am a man of peace, though not a pacifist. In the domain of angling my only enemy is bigotry, which is the offspring of conceit. All kinds of flies and fly-rods are good; but some are better than others. Which is which (and who's who) each angler must find out for himself.

All open-minded anglers will admit that the primary purpose and function of the fly-rod, the cause and aim of its being, philosophically speaking, is to catch fish. If it will not do that, in a hand that knows how to use it, common sense and ethics condemn it to the limbo of foolish and futile contraptions.

The angler who professes not to care what he catches is either a silly fellow or a posing prig. Why go out for fish if you don't want them? Why not take a vanity-case or a portable gramophone with you, instead of a rod? Nothing could be more absurd than the lofty non-piscatorial attitude in an angler.

The first merit of a good fly-rod, from the practical point of view, is that it will enable a man who understands it, and sticks to it through a season on a salmon-river or a trout-stream, to take more game-fish than any kind of bait-rod that ever was built or cut in the woods. This is a fact which I have tested by experience in Norway, Canada, the Tyrol, and various parts of the United States and the United Kingdom.

The hoary legend of the country urchin with a lamming pole, a few yards of twine, and a hideous hookful of bait, who brings home bigger strings of trout every day than all the fly-fishermen, is mythical—an ill-founded flattery of the democracy! It may happen "once in a blue moon." Anything may happen in that lunatic time. *But through a normal season "fine and far off" is the way to take game-fish in fresh waters, and the fly-rod is the chosen implement.*

Consider the delicate and subtle processes of intelligence and skill by which it has been evolved from pristine rudeness to its present perfection. The bunch of red wool with two cock's hackles attached, which served as the first artificial fly, was cast on the rivers of Macedon (where, according to Ælian and William Radcliffe, fly-fishing is first mentioned as practised), by a pole six feet long. Then came various refinements and improvements as set forth in the books of Walton and Cotton, Barker and Venables, and other ingenious spirits of the seventeenth century—a great era. The next century seems to me rather like an interval of torpor in the evolution of the fly-rod. Too fantastic or too brutal, those eighteenth-century fellows; too much occupied with fashion or fighting or philosophic kite-flying, to care for the simple and gentle art of angling. What use had Marlborough or "Hell-Fire" Wharton, Chesterfield or Rousseau or Beau Nash, for a fly-rod?

But with the romantic revival and the splendid Victorian age a great spurt in the evolution of the rod occurred. New woods—the springy lancewood, the tough and flexible greenheart, the temperamental bethabara—were discovered and utilized. No better fundamentally, perhaps, than the familiar hickory or ash, but lighter and more adaptable. The fly-rod lost weight and gained spirit. Then at last, like a long-delayed revelation, came the culminating type of rod—the split-cane as it is called in Britain—the split-bamboo in America. I think bamboo is the better name: more accurate as well as more picturesque. Not every kind of cane will make a good rod. "Bamboo" evokes a vision of those slender, swaying thickets of the Far East—Calcutta and Tonkin—where the pre-destined material for the perfect fly-rod had been growing for so many ages before man developed the sense to use it.

I am sure that some one of the learned contributors to this book is going to tell its readers just where and when the first split-bamboo rod made its appearance. In my little collection of angling books, the first reference that I have found to the use of split-bamboo as a material is in *Frank Forester's Fish and Fishing*, by Henry William Herbert, New York, Stringer and Town-send, 1849 (p. 240). But this refers only to a "tip." When did the complete

[4]

rod first appear? In Britain or in America? Before or after the Crimean War? Frankly, I don't know. Even if I knew I wouldn't tell; for the man who tries to fix that date and the country of origin is certain to get into controversy.

But I am willing to go on to debatable ground far enough to confess my obstinate preference for vegetable material in a fly-rod. Something mineral must be allowed for ferrules, reel-plates and guide-rings. But the less metal the better! The steel fly-rod is a thinly disguised crow-bar. Even the steel centre in a split-bamboo rod feels to me like something dead at the heart of it. Wood is the right material. For wood has been alive in the forest or the thicket, and it still retains some of the grace and resilience of life. It answers kindly to the touch. It springs gladly to obey the will.

Forty years ago a friend of mine (now with God) made me a bamboo trout-rod as a reward for some rambling verses that I wrote about fishing. This sacred rod is 8 feet 6 inches long and weighs 4 ounces. It has three joints, each compacted of eight strips of slender bamboo. 'Tis a shade too limber for a high wind, but perfect in friendly weather. The grip is of sumac wood, beautiful, smooth as silk, but never slippery–delightful to the hand. With that rod I have landed quantities of trout running up to $7\frac{1}{2}$ pounds, and a hantle of salmon from 10 to 20 pounds each. The rod is still alive and ready for action. Just to take it in hand, as I sometimes do in the winter to test its spring in the hall or make a few hookless casts on the lawn, gives me a pleasant thrill of sensation. But far beyond that is the magic by which it recalls beautiful scenes, good companions, useful lessons, and happy days.

Here we come to the *maxima* of the fly-rod. *It is a wand of enchantment; a revealer of secrets; a guide to rivers of Eden; a teacher of the wisdom that is pure, peaceable, and easy to be entreated.*

But before we go on to these greater things, a few more words must be written about the primals–that is to say, the fitness of the rod to cast the fly and to land the fish. Here I hold to the Aristotelian precept of the golden mean. Too much rod makes the angler a toiling slave; too little leaves him helpless in the wind and impotent in playing a fish.

The first salmon-rod I ever owned was bought in Montreal, nearly fifty years ago, on my way to join a friend who had invited me to fish with him on the Restigouche. How long the Canadian tackle-dealer had had it in stock he did not tell me; but he confessed that he was willing to sell it at a reduced price. This tempted me, and I fell. It was a monstrous two-handed engine, made in Edinburgh: three joints of ash and a tip of whalebone; 18 feet long and weighing, I should think, 4 or 5 pounds. It could fling a long line; but it had a "kick" in it that almost threw me out of the canoe every time I cast. No wind could baffle it, no fish could break it, but a day's fishing with it nearly broke my back. It now rests from its labours in a rod-trunk beside the Ste. Marguerite River in Quebec. In guns, fly-rods, and beverages, a "kick" may be a vice!

But I cannot altogether agree with the modernist tendency to extreme lightness in rods. Of course, if you are a sportsman you want to give your fish a fair chance in a fight. *But you may minimise your rod so far that the fish plays you instead of you playing the fish.*

A 2-ounce trout-rod is merely a pretty toy. A one-handed 8-ounce salmon-rod on a sporting river is often a melancholy mockery. On a lake or a long, still pool it will serve. But on a vigorous, lively, temperamental river, where you hardly ever kill your salmon in the pool where you hook him, you need a more capable tool. It must be long enough to put your fly where you want it; heavy enough for the fish to feel it and fight against it instead of merely lolling around in the water; and it must have backbone enough to lift the line over the rocks when your salmon is running down a feather-white rapid "with the bit in his teeth."

Your salmon! But is he really yours? Not yet. The canoe darts down swift channels between rocks that boil with foam. The fish rolls over in the fierce current, rushing this way and that way among the big boulders, a long line out, the reel screaming. *"Debout, m'sieu!"* shout the guides. "Stan' up. Leeft ze rod!" It is difficult and a bit dangerous; but you do it, and the peril is past for the moment. Now the fish halts his rush for the sea and hides in an eddy behind a huge rock. The line is slack. It is you who shouts this time. *"Arrêtez le canot!"* The guides hold the quivering canoe with their setting poles while you turn the reel furiously to take up the line. Then the salmon, like a giant refreshed, makes another long run, or dodges from eddy to eddy, or leaps high in air, or dashes up stream, or crosses the river—a dangerous manœuvre this, for it changes the tension of the line, and the hook may drop out of the hole it has worn. So the battle goes on, perhaps for an hour or more; the canoe swaying, jumping, swerving through the foam, bumping now and then on a hidden rock; the guides shouting to each other as they shove or check the boat with their poles; you with your attention fixed on the bend of your rod, the length of the line run out, the free working of the reel; humouring your tentative fish as much as you dare, but seizing every chance to press a little harder; anxious all the time lest one of a hundred unforeseeable accidents may release the salmon or wreck the canoe.

At last your fish is tired. He swings into a bit of slow water, 20 or 30 feet long, close to the shore, and shows his silver side. You can see him clearly—30 pounds, perhaps more, for he is thick across the shoulders. He is ready to be lifted into the boat with the gaff, or with the "tailer," which is better because it does not mar the fish. A sharp tap on the head with the wooden "priest" ends his struggles. Now he is really yours. Lucky that your rod had backbone enough for that difficult job!

[6]

Now, if you are a strenuous fisherman, you will hurry back to the pool where you hooked that fish, and try to get another. But if you are an easy-going person, caring more for the pleasure of your pastime than for the pride of your angling record, you will seek a pretty place on the shady bank of the river, and go ashore for a bit of lunch with your guides, who are also your friends. Kindle a small fire to broil the bacon and toast the good *habitant* bread made from whole wheat flour. How sweet and wholesome it tastes! How refreshing the hot tea, or the cup which cheers but does not inebriate, when mixed with a dash of highland dew! Now you can light your pipe and meditate *de maximis* of the fly-rod.

Do you remember all the lovely streams to which it has introduced you? I can recall to "my mind's eye" every brook or little river (and almost every lake) on which I have cast the fly. The flowing waters are far and away the best. They are full of life and unexpectedness. Each bend and turn has a surprise of beauty. They lead you on and on into enchanted places. They sing to you as they flow. No music is more sweet and soothing than the onward voice of running waters.

What wild flowers grow along their banks, changing with the seasons, so that you need no calendar to tell you what time of year it is! Arbutus, anemones, and moccasin-flowers in the spring; mountain-laurel and rhododendron in June; tall meadow-rue and wood-lilies in midsummer; golden-rod and purple asters and sky-blue gentians in early autumn. Why are the flowers of the rowan-tree snow-white and its berries coral-red? There must be magic in it. Colour is a gift of heaven to earth. Fragrance is an extra gift.

Then there are the birds: rare in the depths of the forest, more plentiful on the banks of a little river, most abundant along the course of a meandering trout-stream. How very much alive they are—

"the most alive of living things"—

and how companionable to the quiet-moving, meditative angler! In God's name, what makes them sing so much? Yes, I think that's it: they sing in God's name. In Britain you have your famous friends: the skylark, the song-thrush, the nightingale, the blackbird, the linnet, the redbreast. In America we have different names and songs: the veery, the hermit-thrush, the rose-breasted grosbeak, the oriole, the Maryland yellow-throat, the song-sparrow, the fox-sparrow, the purple finch, and half a hundred kinds of warblers. There is no better way of becoming acquainted with them than to follow the magical guidance of the fly-rod.

Moreover, it has philosophic lessons to teach, secrets of life to reveal.

Do you recall the first time you tried to handle it? How you struggled to get your fly out, to *make* it go where you wanted it to go? How you pushed it, and brandished it, and used your arm and back to force it? How the light-feathered

[7]

hook refused to obey you, went tangling among the tree-branches, fell close to your feet, or flopped anywhere on the water? It seemed hopeless until a wise voice said to you: "Use your rod, laddie; take your time, and let your rod do the work." Then by slow degrees, and more by example than by precept, you learned the first secret of the art. It is a slight movement of the forearm and wrist that calls the rod to pick the fly from the water, sends it behind you in a long, easy curve, and then springs it forward again to the chosen spot where the trout is rising. It is the spring of your rod that does the work. But you must give it time as well as guidance. Otherwise it will snap your fly off on the back-cast with a crack like a whip.

Persuasion is better than force. Time may be only a mental form, but it is a factor in all good work. Reforms fail because reformers forget to allow for the backcast.

This begins to sound like preaching. I must break it off. Anglers of the old school will tolerate a little of that kind of thing when their pipes are going—but not too much! So here is my last word *de maximis* of the fly-rod.

Its greatest gifts are the friends it makes for you. Quiet people, contented people, fond of mirth and music, pleased with small mercies, full of patience and goodwill. My father was the first of these I knew; since then the fly-rod has brought many good comrades. Brothers of the angler, an old brother salutes you. Here or yonder, wheresoe'er ye wander, fare ye well!

CHAPTER II

by

William Radcliffe

"OUT OF MACEDONIA"

"Oh! for a perfect day in June
In a quiet place with mind in tune!
Just to lie still while the hours run,
Musing, and dreaming, and drunk with sun!"

TO the fog-numbed London poet the presence of all his conditions on our river in Norway, save that the month was late July and that the boom of the shrunken Foss was still heard in the land, would have brought joyous satisfaction. Not so, however, to my cousin and myself (obliged to leave for England in three days), as the water, always gin-like because of clarification in its two lake sources, had now, owing to drought and constant sunshine, become so low and so crystal clear that even my eyes could detect movements of fish, whose more powerful lenses enabled them to spot instantly the slightest stir in or over the stream.

Against such conditions we, Apostle-like, had toiled for many days and caught, if not naught, little. "The Pool of Silence" alone yielded an infrequent fish. There, when low water forbids ascent of the Foss, the salmon lie in meditative manner varied by an occasional leap into the air. But for years past no cast however deft, no fly however coloured, had effected even a "feather rise," until my cousin, equipped with very light tackle and tiny dry flies, devised the plan of waiting near a rock island or bank till a splash beckoned the boat silently to glide far enough for a fly to reach the centre of the spreading rings. Then sometimes the philosophic recluse changed instantly into an astounded but "bonnie fechter."

To the Pool I made my way one sultry, cloudless, windless afternoon, hopeless of success, and worried by a reminder from our editor that my chapter must shortly reach him.

Not one of the leaping fish, although my fly often settled lightly among the splash's rings, deigned to notice it. In vain had I thrice chanted the prayer to Ninā, the Babylonian goddess of the waters, meaning " May the fisher catch many fish! May the goddess grant as her gift that he this day prosper!"*

Twice did I imitate, but unsuccessfully, the Chinese Hsü, whose custom "was while drinking and fishing by turns, to pour out a libation, accompanied by 'Drink, too, ye Spirits of the River!' " Hsü's creel, invariably full even when others were empty, testified to their gratitude, which was evidenced by one of them, touched, perhaps even affected, by the alcoholic libation, each night gliding down stream, quietly driving the lower reaches and shepherding the fishes to Hsü's bait.

Yielding at last to my surroundings, I actualised our poet's two last lines, save changing his "drunk with" to "damning sun." My "musing" ran on angling from Homer to Ælian, marred by the intrusive King Charles's head of the editor's letter, since frequent cudgelling of my so-called mind in quest of matter or even title for my article had dismally failed. But, "musing and dreaming," I was awakened by a flop of a fish and found myself murmuring, "Oh! man of Macedonia, come over and help us!"

The effect was instantaneous: the inert changed to the alert mind, and both matter and title shone out as clear as an electric sign, for as blessed as "Mesopotamia" to the old lady was "Macedonia" to me.

As the "gentle reader," an such exist in the twentieth century, may well wonder how this inversion of the Pauline S.O.S. (see Acts xvi. 9) wrought this miracle, let me explain that "Macedonia" conjured before me the wraiths of no lesser men than Alexander the Great, his tutor Aristotle, our own Shakespeare, and, most important, Ælian, *homo classicus* of the first artificial fly, etc.

(Here, *en parenthèse*, may I add that possibly by the spirit of one of the dwellers on the River Astræus investing my dry fly with the virtue of his primitive artificial, or perhaps by my two libations at last getting their work in, I killed three fish, and so for once on reaching home was not greeted by Martial's taunt, *"Ecce redit sporta piscator inani"*?)

* My friend Dr. Langdon, Professor of Assyriology at Oxford, has since informed me that the prayer was offered on behalf of netting and commercial fishing, as is shown by (*inter alia*) "May the fish-market at Babylon always be well-stocked!" Since on our river fly-casting alone prevails, the local Lady of the Water may well have resented such association and thus remained deaf to my entreaties. The omission from the Norse Pantheon of any God of Fishing excites surprise when we recall its frequent mention in connection not only with men but also with gods–*e.g.*, Thor's using as a bait for the Midhgarhd the head of an ox, and the invention (according to the Icelandic *Sagas*) of the net by Loki, originally the God of Fire.

The first three, if less pertinent to *The Book of the Fly-Rod*, are yet from their connection with or references to fishes and fishing fully entitled to mention.

ALEXANDER THE GREAT

The chief claim of Alexander rests on the statement of Pliny (*N.H.* viii., 17) that by placing at the disposal of Aristotle (the influence of whose teaching was manifest all through his career) several thousand men to collect fishes and animals from the then known world, he enabled him to produce his famous *Natural History*, to finish which (according to Athenæus) he added 800 talents.

For Pliny's statement, backed only by much later writers, we possess (as I have shown elsewhere*) not one scrap of internal evidence. This, indeed, manifests that nearly all the fishes and animals with which Aristotle was practically acquainted belonged to Greece or Western Asia, and in most part to Lesbos, where he lived for four years.

Alexander (as Arrian, *Indica* 26, tells) was deeply interested in the Ichthyophagi (of the Persian Gulf) encountered on his Indian expedition. He found them denied the ordinary sources of subsistence by the barrenness of their country, and thus compelled to use fish for *every* purpose–food, clothes, houses etc.†–and as they were, from the nature of this their only food, very short-lived, though comparatively free from disease, he forbade and took steps to vary their unmixed diet.

ARISTOTLE

Aristotle owes his inclusion here to his *History of Animals*, written in all probability during his seven years' sojourn in Macedonia, whither he went straight from his study of fishes etc. in Sappho's Lesbos. In this great work, a mere by-product, so to speak, of his stupendous brain, he enumerates of fishes alone at least 110, mostly given without any real attempt at classification or adequate description. Although in many instances he discusses the anatomical characteristics, food, breeding habits, migrations, and modes of capture, of the 110 only some 50 can be scientifically identified, of which all save 6 come from the sea.

Even if his ideas of specific distinction were as vague as those of the fishermen whose nomenclature he adopted, the fact cannot be gainsaid that Aristotle still remains a very great naturalist as well as a very great biologist, despite his apparent lack of any aseptic preparation for the preservation of his specimens.

This figure of 110 speaks wonders for his industry and knowledge, for even

---

* *Fishing from the Earliest Times*, 2nd edition, 1926, p. 110.
† Marco Polo (iii. 41) states that the Ichthyophagi of Arabia fed their cattle, camels, and horse with dried fish on which they throve.

after the lapse of the 1,800 years separating him from the sixteenth century the list of Mediterranean fishes compiled by Belon comprises but some 100, and by Rondelet some 160, names.

Little escaped his ken or pen. He was the first to point out that by its scales it is possible to make a shrewd (in the case of the gasteropod mollusc, the *Murex*, an exact) computation of the aging of a fish. "The *Murex* lives for about six years, and the yearly increase is indicated by a distinct interval in the spiral convolution of the shell " (v. 15). Leeuwenhoek (the discoverer in the eighteenth century of scale-reading, which reveals the ages of fish) states that in the examination by "a rough self-made microscope" of the scales of a large 40-year-old carp he counted the component *scale-layers* lying one above the other "as if glued together," and found without exception that a new layer larger than the one of the preceding year is annually added.

Had microscopes existed in Aristotle's day, may we not surmise that he would have done more than foreshadow scale-reading, and thus have come down to posterity with his title of "The Philosopher of the Many Rings," better earned than by his foppish affection for jewellery?

He notes that (1) "The *tunny* more than any other fish delights in the heat of the sun" (viii. 19).

(2) "The *skaros* is the only fish which seems to ruminate" (ii. 17), and its teeth did not interlock like those of other fish, but resembled, as did its beak, those of a parrot (ii. 13).

(3) "The *octopus* clings so tightly to the rocks that it cannot be pulled off, even when the knife is used to sever it : and yet if one employ flea-bane (κόνυζα) to the creature, it drops off at once" (iv. 8), an end now attained in Greece by employing tobacco.

(4) "The *scolopendra*, after swallowing the hook, turns itself inside out until it has ejected it and then again turns outside in" (ii. 17).

The above are but a few of the many traits and tricks of fishes recounted in his *Natural History*. The author held that fishes possessed the sense of hearing (iv. 8) and of smell, but denied them that of *voice* (with the doubtful exception of the *dolphin*), while allowing them the making of noises fully treated in iv. 9.

But even the accurate Aristotle, like Homer, "sometimes nods," and so badly that the Comedians, fastening on such a lapse as that the whole race of shell-fish generate without connection, dubbed him "a very wonder unto fools." He blundered badly, too, in his statement as to the propagation of eels, when, misled by their apparent lack of generative organs, milt and roe, he asserted that they sprang from the so-called "entrails of the earth" or certain worms formed in the mud. Similarly, in the 2,200 years necessary till Dr. Johann Schmidt solved this *crux* in the twentieth century, many others blundered in their attribution of origin to the dews of the May mornings! the hairs of horses! the gills of fish! and last—our Izaak Walton's view—spontaneous generation!

It is curious to recall that Aristotle, though apparently familiar with most of the then existent methods of fishermen, even telling about the best lures and "luckiest hours" for taking certain fish, makes no mention of *actual* fishing, save in his story of the fight with and escape of a big fresh-water fish, the *glanis* (vi. 13).

SHAKESPEARE

"Que diable," I hear a reader querying, *"allait-il faire dans cette galère?"* Because of his lines in *Henry V.*, Act iv., Scene 7.

GOWER: O, 'tis a gallant king.

FLUELLEN: Ay, he was porn at Monmouth, Captain Gower. What call you the town's name where Alexander the pig was porn?

GOWER: Alexander the Great.

FLUELLEN: Why, I pray you, is not pig great?

GOWER: I think Alexander the Great was born in Macedon.

FLUELLEN: I tell you, Captain, if you look in the maps of the 'orld I warrant you shall find in the comparisons between Macedon and Monmouth that the situations, look you, is both alike. There is a river in Macedon and there is also, moreover, a river at Monmouth. It is called the Wye at Monmouth, but it is out of my prains what is the name of the other river, but 'tis all one; 'tis like as my fingers is to my fingers, and there is salmons in both.

In an article in 1926 entitled "And there is salmons in both," I showed that this statement (occurring in the famous but fatuous parallel between Alexander the Great and Henry V.) is incorrect, because in no river in Macedon nor in any influent of the Mediterranean (probably on account of too high a temperature) can be found *Salmo salar* or *Salmo trutta*, an assertion which Day, Gunther, Moreau, and Da Silva confirm.

Why did Shakespeare put the words into Fluellen's mouth? From sheer ignorance or from design to make the "learned quiddity of Welsh pedants," whom he rarely misses the chance of ridiculing (*e.g.*, Evans, in *The Merry Wives of Windsor*), still more fatuous? I inclined to the first alternative, because (according to H. N. Ellacombe) Shakespeare, although "probably an expert with most English fish, never refers to salmon *fishing*," an omission which from his months spent on or near Severn and the Wye seems for such an observant pen astonishing. Indeed, to judge from the only reference in his works to the fish (*Othello*, Act ii., Scene 1, line 155), he seems only interested in the salmon as a comestible:

> "She that in wisdom never was so frail
> To change the cod's head for the salmon's tail."

[15]

Given for the purpose of the parallel the necessity of a river in Macedon, did Shakespeare infer (as did a very learned authority in the last century) the existence of Macedonian salmon from the passage, famous as the first mention of an artificial fly, in Ælian, *Natural History*, xv. 1? He could have read it, if not in an English, in the Latin translations by Gesner in 1556 and by Gillius in 1562, as W. Theobald (*The Classical Elements in Shakespeare's Plays*) deems likely from four other passages, which he persuasively attributes to Ælian's influence.

Sir Herbert Maxwell followed, "acquitting him alike of error in ichthyology and making a butt of Fluellen," because while admitting my statement that there is no *Salmo salar* nor *trutta* in Mediterranean waters, "some of them contain plenty of fish of the genus *Salmo*, which it is difficult to distinguish either in appearance or the quality of their flesh from the Atlantic salmon." In support he, "though unacquainted with the rivers of Macedon," instanced as coming from the Lake of Scutari and from the River Moraca such-like fishes "of which Shakespeare may well have heard from travellers or sailors."

To any reply (as to so many other pleasant diversions) the General Strike put an end here, but in U.S.A. my article (published in *Outdoor America*) evoked much controversy as to how such fish should be properly classed. Finally, that learned ichthyologist, Dr. L. A. Adams, of the University of Illinois, decided, after examination of the works of the foremost zoologists, that both Sir Herbert Maxwell and I could be held to be right, and concluded with, "What is the exact relation of the Scutari fish and Danube *Hucho* to the genus *Salmo* is one of the intricate problems of classification that makes the gray hairs come early in the workers of science."

I would have been content to leave the matter thus had not our greatest British authority, Mr. Tate Regan, permitted me to quote from a letter (July 9, 1930). "There are no salmon or sea trout in the Mediterranean. The fish of Lake Scutari are, I believe, *S. trutta*. The most salmon-like fish in the Mediterranean (in structure, not in size) is *S. obtusirosis*" (with which he deals in *Salmon and Trout Magazine*, June, 1920, p. 28). "I take it that by salmon is meant *S. salar*, and by Macedonia not the Danube, etc. It would be far-fetched to say that Shakespeare was right because he was thinking of barbel in the Tigris!"

Had this Macedonian salmon been merely another Shakespearian error like that of his Bohemian sea-coast, I should have kept silence. But, as I found that the mischief wrought by "there is salmons in both" was still at work, and the author of (to my mind) the very best book on a certain province of fishing, and a very omniscient law lord, were both gravely infected, I entered my warning against the danger in England, and added for like purpose in U.S.A. the following:

Plate IV

"But the mischief workable in the near future by Shakespeare's error, unless proclaimed *urbi et orbi*, to my eye looms large. From America alone I can descry bands of passionate pilgrims enticed under false pretences to Macedon. First hurries my friend Dr. Henry van Dyke, with the 'urge' to add an Astræan to his incomparable *Tales of Little Rivers*. Next my friend Mr. Zane Grey, with a specially devised electric contraption, which can not only turn on a tenth of its own axis, but can jump waterfalls (he will surely with pure Santa Catalina *water* christen his boat 'Salmo,' meaning 'the leaper'), and can like a submarine or Brer Fox 'lay low,' so as to include among his goodly stock of world's records a Bercœan. Lastly, behold Mr. Hewett and Mr. La Branche! The first with a rod, almost diaphanous and weightless, yet capable of dealing death to so fierce a fighter as a vagrant *Parasilurus aristotelis*. The second arrives with a minute dry fly (dressed as Ælian *postea* describes), destined, perhaps, to become as immortal as its Thessalonican prototype."

ÆLIAN

For Ælian's inclusion no explanation is needed, for to him the gratitude of all who ply the fly-rod must always flow, since in the account in his *Natural History*, xv. 1, occurs the very first specific mention and description in all ancient literature of an artificial fly. And not only is he the first, but also (with one possible exception) the only author in some 1,300 years, who makes any reference to such a fly. After him (*c.* A.D. 130) till Dame Juliana Berners (*Treatyse of Fysshynge with an Angle*, 1496) we find neither mention of nor allusion to it, but that it was then a well-known method of angling is easily deduced from the authoress's abrupt introduction of the subject, "These ben xij flies or dubbes with which ye shall angle"–which is a precept of practice rather than a revelation of invention.

If the usually accurate *Bibliotheca Piscatoria* be right that Ælian's account–of such intense interest to anglers–"was first pointed out by Stephen Oliver in 1834," it must have remained unknown or unnoticed in England for no less a period than seventeen centuries.

For reasons of space I abridge or paraphrase the original. "I have heard of a Macedonian way of catching fish: in a river called the Astræus are fish of speckled colouring.* They feed on flies about the size of "the flowery one" or wild bee†–peculiar to the country and quite unlike those found elsewhere–

---

* Why does Ælian, while carefully giving the local name for the flies (Hippouroi, or Horsetails), refer us to "the people of the country" for the name of the fish? Probably because they were trout, for which in Greek there seems no recognised name. Pausanias (viii. 21, 2) terms similar fish elsewhere ποικιλίαι, or speckled.

† *Anthedon*, probably one of the *Syrphidæ*.

E

"which hover about the river and settle on it in search of their food." When a fish detects a fly floating on the surface, "he swims very quietly and coming up when close to its shadow snaps it down. But anglers never use these natural flies," for if handled their natural colour is lost, their wings get crushed, and the fish refuse them. "So they wrap crimson red wool round a hook and tie on to it two feathers which grow under a cock's wattles and resemble wax in colour. Their rod is 6 foot long and their line the same." When they throw their lure, a fish attracted by the colour rises madly, "thinking that the pretty thing will yield him a dainty mouthful, but on opening his jaws he is caught by the hook and enjoys a bitter repast, a captive!"

Of the numerous points of interest arising from the above, I confine myself to two:

(a) Was the Macedonian artificial fly a "new invention" as most fishing writers have acclaimed it?

(b) What was the length and material of the ancient rods?

The Fly

(a) I have elsewhere maintained that so far from being a "new invention," or even a striking departure from known methods, the fly merely instances the Macedonian's adaptability to his environment and his imitative skill in dressing (as do his descendants today) a fly resembling that on which the fish were feeding. Had it been an "invention," would Ælian, to whose familiarity with methods of fishing his *Natural History* testifies, have simply confined himself to "I have heard of a Macedonian way of fishing, and it is this"? No! this passage heralded in no "invention," but lays much stress on a special, local, and improved adaptation of a known device–in a word, as *le dernier cri* in flies!

In support of my assertion I adduce first, *Natural History*, xv. 10, which pictures fishing in the sea for pelamyds when the flies must have been artificial. A man in the stern of a rowed boat lets out on each side a line carrying hooks, all of which bear lures made of crimson wound round at intervals by white wool, and with a seamew's (probably small) feather attached so as to flutter gently in the water–a passable resemblance to some modern salmon flies and a method not unlike exaggerated harling.

Second, xiv. 22, the *thymalus* in the Italian river Ticinus could not be caught on a hook baited "with pig's fat, winged ant, shell fish, fish gut," or anything except the κώνωψ, probably mosquito, to judge from its description as "that horrid insect, a foe to man both day and night alike with his buzz and his bite." Dr. A. J. Butler,* to meet the difficulty (pressed previously by me)

* *Sport in Classic Times*, 1930, p. 171, a work by a fine scholar and expert angler, from which I borrow freely.

[18]

of any ancient hook being small enough to impale a mosquito, suggests that the successful lure was an artificial fly, dressed, perhaps, larger than the natural model.

Third, Martial (some half-century before Ælian), *Ep.* v. 18, where the first mention (now that *musca,* and not *musco,* is the accepted reading) of any *fishing* fly occurs.

> Odi dolosas munerum et malas artes.
> Imitantur hamos dona: namque quis nescit
> Avidum vorata decipi scarum musca?

From his employing it as an illustration, not drawing attention to the novelty of such use, and especially from the words *"quis nescit?"* which imply a general knowledge, fly fishing seems to have been a long invented and common method.

Two reasons strongly incline me to the presumption that Martial's fly was artificial. (1) The purpose, especially of the first line and a half, is to inveigh against fraudful gifts or all things presented which are not what they appear, typical of which fraudful flies are instanced, and (2) the difficulty which the Romans would have experienced in impaling without damaging a natural fly on one of their hooks,* and further of fastening it securely enough to withstand the buffets of the sea, would have exceeded the skill of the best of Homer's "craftsmen, welcome over all the wide earth."

These four instances, two in the sea and two in rivers in places far remote one from another, seem to prove that the artificial fly was widely used before Ælian's and probably Martial's time. But when Dr. Butler† contends that because in the Astræus (with its peculiar breed of fish) the angler on account of the shortness of the rod and line must have kept his fly *floating,* "we have here the first authentic instance of *dry-fly* fishing," I must demur. For, if it be "a far cry to Lochaber," it is a far, far longer from *c.* 130 to the first (Pulman's) dry fly in 1851.

The Rod—Its Length and Nature

(*b*) Does the measurement of 6 feet in length (given *supra*) apply to the ancient rods generally? "To ask such an absurd question is to answer it," I can hear a reader mutter. So thought I originally, but research changed my view, for it established as a fact that from the first-known angling scene at Beni Hasan (Egypt) *c.* 2000 B.C. down to A.D. 500, we can find in ancient art not one single rod or line at all approaching modern length and rarely one ex-

---

* The smallest hook in the Greek-Roman (Amathus) collection at the British Museum measures over ¼ inch in breadth at the bend.

† *Op. cit.,* 167.

ceeding the 4 cubits or 6 feet, which Ælian (the only author, as far as I know, who gives any dimensions) expressly states was its length. Against this fact it was contended that I did not allow sufficiently for artistic convention or the exigencies on vases (where for long the decorative *motif* was uppermost) of the artist's space, which forbade the representation of a long rod in just proportion to the height of the angler without unduly reducing in scale his, the really important, figure.

I countered (1) by asking if in Greek ceramic art spears and rods of athletic trainers admittedly bear a true proportion to the rest of the picture, why should not rods of modern size? "Because the first can, while the second can not, be got into the picture," came the reply. But, I continued, if on the exterior of red-figured *kraters*, etc., the artist often allows the end of a spear, etc., to run outside the limits of his panel or marginal pattern, why not a similar treatment of rods? I grant that conventional size has to be reckoned in landscape accessories (trees, buildings, etc.) on a diminished scale to form a back- or even a fore- ground. The important details of a myth (*e.g.*, the crab in Hercules *v.* the hydra) may be exaggerated for clearness or emphasis, but the deliberate misrepresentation of a common article surely belongs to a different category.

One devotee of the conventional objection carried his zeal so far as to waive Ælian aside by, "Perhaps he was wrong." Perhaps, but till this can be proved I must abide by his definite measurements as locally and generally correct, although *vis-à-vis* with the use in *Od.* xii. 251 *f.*, and in Oppian of long rods (both, however, be it noted, in the sea), I admit that these did not apply universally.

What was the exact material and nature of rods in classic times still remains an insoluble question, but Dr. Butler* has by his wide research added much to our knowledge and by his "intelligent anticipation of coming events" to our interest. For Homer's "long rod" the bamboo has usually been accepted, though wrongly because it was not indigenous in Greece and can hardly have been imported in his time.

From Pliny† we learn that for fishing-rods the *arundo* from Abaris in Africa is *laudatissima*. This Ælian‡ distinguishes from the *narthex* (which has to be polished) and from cornel wood. The former corresponds to the *ferula*, a kind of reed from which a light cane rod might easily have been made. To these two Dr. Butler adds the *arundo donax*, a native of the Mediterranean and by far the largest of European reeds, and concludes that this furnished the Greeks and Romans with a long and the *ferula* with a shorter and whippier rod.

Although Ælian seems the first to mention a *rod* of cornel, from Pliny's description of the wood's slenderness and toughness Dr. Butler§ deduces that it

* *Op. cit.*, 136-9.　　† *Natural History*, xxi. 66.　　‡ xii. 43.　　§ *Op. cit.*, 138.

supplied a rod far stronger and more powerful than any weapon of reed—"in fact, a *greenheart rod*, which, though it did not supersede the angler's lighter cane rod, greatly widened the sphere of his art and increased his pleasure." This making greenheart an alternative to cornel is quite wrong, because the former grows only in the West Indies and South America, and thus could not have been known to the Greeks and Romans.*

Ten years ago in considering Martial's (*Ep.*, xiv. 219)

"Callida dum tacita crescit arundo manu,"

I wrote that there was used before Martial's time a *reed* rod capable of extension either by protruding a smaller cane through a larger one or else by an action somewhat similar to a chimney sweep's, with jointed rods fastened together in the hand, when prolonging his brush. Further, I asked, if such rod was of service to the fowler for reaching a bird on a high branch, is it not almost certain that despite no express mention ("Silence precludyth not presence") the angler employed a similar rod for getting his lure or bait over intervening obstacles and increasing the length of his throw?

To my authorities Dr. Butler† adds *Anth. Pal.*, vi. 192, and Bion, iv. 5 (who lived some 300 years before Martial), and claims that "we have not only carried back the use of the jointed rod to *c.* 250 B.C., and have proved its use from one end of the Mediterranean to the other, but also its use *for fishing* as well as fowling."

Readers of *The Book of the Fly-Rod* will surely realise the enduring love of angling throughout the ages and from one at least of these four men "out of Macedonia" will, I trust, visualise the angler of some nineteen centuries ago setting forth with tackle worse but with hope equal to his descendant's of to-day to disprove (proleptically) De Quincey's "fishing is an unceasing expectation and a perpetual disappointment" by breaking his own and all other records.

* The first known greenheart rod, made by Mr. G. Kelson, appeared only *c.* 1850.
† *Op. cit.*, 188-9.

CHAPTER III

by

G. E. M. Skues

IF WE STARTED AFRESH

THE accumulation of error and misconception which has grown up round the art of trout-fishing with the fly during the centuries of its evolution is so bewildering that it would perhaps conduce to the clearing of one's mind if one could throw overboard all the lore of the past, and start afresh—endeavouring to see how, if there had never been any art of fishing with the fly, it might be brought into being by a new and unprejudiced mind, equipped, of course, with some capacity of observation and of deducing sound conclusions from its observations, also some acquaintance with modern science, particularly optics.

One might assume that one's observer, passing from time to time by a trout-stream, had seen the surface broken by the rise of fish; had seen the insects floating down the surface and then sucked in; had at other times seen a seemingly precisely similar incident occur with no insect on the surface; had been intrigued by the difference, and stimulated to solve the problem of that difference.

Let us suppose him, then, to have set to work, and to have secured one or more trout. His first step would be to open the fish or to force a wet marrow spoon down its gullet, and to float the contents of each stomach in a basin or plate of white china, or perhaps better, in a thin glass vessel, of the quality used by analytical chemists, preferably four-sided instead of round. With the latter our observer could hold the stomach contents up to the light and see not only their shapes and colours and whether they were winged or subaqueous in form, but also their several degrees of translucency, though he could deduce the same facts almost as conclusively if the background employed were white china.

Having got so far, it would not be a great step to think of using the insects which he has observed as forming the food of the trout as hook bait. Nor would it take him very long to realise that with the exception, perhaps, of caddis worms, and possibly mayflies, all the insects are too tender in their make-up to remain on a hook, however tiny, to say nothing of their being too small.

The next step in our observer's mental processes is a big one–but we must assume that he takes it, for in the past someone has taken the step of realising that the fly food of the trout may be artificially simulated on a hook. Perhaps he may have seen a trout slash a feather drifting from a branch of a tree on to the surface. Once, however, the idea is caught that fly life can be simulated by feathers, the prospect of progress widens rapidly under the stimulus of a new idea. Our observer spends much time in the poultry markets, examining the feathers of various birds and comparing the relative translucency of their fibres. Picking up a moulted starling primary or secondary wing feather and laying it over writing or print, he must have been struck by the way in which it is possible to read through it. Holding it up to the light he will have been struck by its prismatic radiance. And he will have been led to compare other similar feathers with it, such as the primaries of blackbird (cock and hen), thrush, and fieldfare. He will have seen that the denser feathers, such as land-rail primary and secondary, cock and hen pheasant, and others are more suitable for suggesting the denser tribes of insect such as the sedges. In his attempts to suggest the legs of insects he will have naturally given attention to the hackles of poultry and other birds. The relative soppiness when wetted of hen hackles and the hackles of birds other than poultry will have convinced him of their greater suitableness for the legs of subaqueous life. A little reflection and some comparison with the appearance of winged duns found in the trout's stomach would tell him that in rough and tumbling waters they might well suggest the wings of the perfect insect caught and ruined by the water, while the stiff bright hackles of the dun cock would suggest the wings of the floating spinner cocked or spent.

The bodies of his insects would be his next consideration. The tying silk might in the simpler cases be enough. Floss silk would then be suggested, but he would soon realise the need for some degree of translucency. In order to secure this for his insects the dyed wools from his wife's work-basket would be a fairly obvious step. To spin these on as dubbing would not perhaps occur to him at once unless he were familiar with the processes of cloth manufacture. He would probably try securing one end with the tying silk and winding on the wool. Pulling out a strand for a body, he would often find it presenting a natural taper, and perhaps one day working with very sticky waxed silk it might occur to him to wind the wool round the tying silk before lapping on the body. Once the advantage of this was realised we should have him spinning on the wool systematically. From this course to the use of furs from hare, rabbit, cat, etc., creating an artificial loose taper in the material before apply-

Plate No. 3

ing it to the sticky tying silk would be a short enough step. If he were a natural genius like Mr. J. W. Dunne we might soon find him devising bodies successively of dyed horsehair or gut over the bare shank of an eyed hook. He must ere this have evolved the eyed hook, and gut he would have borrowed from the bottom fisher. Thence we should have him discovering the effect of sheer translucency obtained by winding artificial silks of delicate hues over hook shanks enamelled white. The turning and securing of the hackle would be a mechanical process which would not long elude our competent observer.

He would now be in a position to simulate on a hook most of the insects other than beetles which form the food of the trout. The sheen of the feathers of a peacock's tail would naturally suggest the iridescent surface of a beetle's body.

Once peacock's herl is discovered the way is opened first to the use of other herls, such as heron and goose and swan, for bodies, and to the discovery of the "quill" obtained by stripping the flue from these herls.

With the equipment thus obtained our competent observer is now able to represent almost any insect that forms the food of the trout. He will not, however, be obsessed by any theory of dry fly or wet. He will have realised that the vast bulk of the food of the trout is subaqueous, and, being wise, he will also lay his account with that; but, being so wise, he will also recognise that there are many occasions when the trout are feeding mainly on the surface, and he will be prepared for such occasions by having dressed appropriate flies. He will realise that for the floating fly he must use materials which stand up to a different and harder kind of wear than that which sunken lures undergo.

Having thus attained a view of things derived direct from nature and the study of nature, it would at this stage perhaps do him little harm, and possibly some good, to study the fly-fishing and fly-dressing literature of the past, for it might perhaps provide him with some tips in the way of materials and the use of materials–while his mind would have been fortified by direct contact with the reality of things to detect and reject the errors and false doctrine perpetuated from age to age, with which the literature of the past is full.

Still, for all that, he would only be at the beginning of a great subject, and if he were, as he should be, learned in optics and anatomy he would have much to deduce from the anatomy of the trout's eye, and from optical principles, how the trout sees its food under and over and on the surface, and he might in time take the science or art of trout-fishing a long way beyond the stage which it has at present reached. He would know all about the refraction and reflection of light, all about the trout's window, and all about how the mirror-like underside of the surface film enables the trout to keep the whole field of his under-water world under observation, while at the same time observing the approach of floating insects by the impressions of their feet, bodies, and wings on the surface as well as by observation through his window.

The shrewd reader will, of course, have noticed that our observer has, so far, not dealt with either fly-rods, casting-lines, or gut. As regards gut, he would no doubt borrow from the roach fisher gut of quite sufficient fineness. He would doubtless begin with dapping, for which a stiff rod would prove adequate. But soon the desire to reach fish rising away from the banks would lead him to the use of the blow line, and then to the idea of a rod with sufficient spring in it to carry a line, with the aid of the wind, to the feeding fish. Once the idea of the spring has been mastered, the desire to fish up stream against the wind as well as with the wind, or even to fish in still weather, would lead to the evolution of the stiff casting-rod, the heavy-enough casting-line, its taper, and the tapered gut cast, and thence back to the fly and the cock-winged floater.

One might say that in so doing he would be just where we are now. I say "No." For his artificial insects, both subaqueous and floating and semi-submerged, would bear true relations to the natural insects, not only as they are, but as it may be deduced that the trout sees them. He would not be dressing imitations or representations of the perfect winged insect for fishing under water—but his studies would have enabled him to deduce the general impression which the trout receives of the natural insect, whether floating or subaqueous, and he need never be bothered with any of the string of ridiculous nostrums which crowd the pages of angling writers even to this day. He would dress what he wanted, which would be what the trout wanted, and he would not lose sight of the proper occasions for suggesting in his imitations the mobility of life.

He would know, moreover, that the trout, being a natural born tyrant and bully, will often be attracted by what otherwise appears to be a genuine natural insect acting in an unnatural manner as if it were in distress, or displaying some feature which picks it out from among its apparent fellows as requiring investigation and special attention applied by the only means open to a trout—his extremely capacious maw.

At this stage I think we may leave him till a better man comes along.

CHAPTER IV

by

Arthur Ransome

THE TRAVELLING COMPANION

WHEN rods were made in a single piece, the best of all travelling companions had not yet been discovered. A fisherman on a journey might take a fly or two, a palmer or a bee in his bonnet, a hank of horsehair and some hooks, but he did not take a rod. Aksakov and his father, travelling in Russia, counted on the woods by the river bank to furnish them with rods when they stopped for the night or to bait their horses, and so people do in Russia to this day. Charles Cotton had to lend his guest a rod when he persuaded him to rest a little on the road to Manchester and angle a trout or two out of the Dove. Perhaps he had to do as much for Walton, though Walton speaks so lovingly of rods (he had one top, he says, that lasted him twenty years) that he may have had long joints stained green with verdegris slung behind him when he went north from London. Dame Juliana herself wrote of a jointed rod, but praised it chiefly for its craftiness. It was a rod "so preuy that ye may walke therwyth: and there shall noo man wyte where abowte yee goo." The jointed rod was known in England long ago, but it was not until those changes came about that have turned us all to nomads, not until stage coaches and then railways were invented to carry us rapidly from river to river, that the fisherman and his rod became inseparable. Macadam and then Stephenson had a good deal to do with it. It is not quite a hundred years since Stephen Oliver (who travelled by coach from London to the north, where alone he thought it worth while to fish) advised the fisherman to fit his rod with a belt so that on a long walk (for he was to be independent of coaches when he came to the country of the Yore and the Lune) he might "sling it like a rifle." The fisherman was to carry a walking-stick into which he could screw a large hook for a gaff. He was to wrap an extra shirt and a pair of stockings in oilskin, pilot-fashion, and to stuff them in his creel, while carrying a volume of Wordsworth in his pocket. The other volumes were to be in the travelling trunk, which, with a change of clothes and a few more shirts, he was to send on by the carrier. His dress was to be that of "a plain, single-minded man, who for a while laying aside the artificial distinctions of society, was willing to pass among his fellow-men at his own intrinsic value." The material of his clothes was to be of a light texture. On no account was he to wear velveteens, fustian, or moleskin for—heroic days!—"should he have to swim a mile or two—across Bassenthwaite or Ullswater to save going six miles about—he would find them a serious weight when thoroughly saturated with water."

There, at last, is the fishing-rod beginning to take its proper place as its owner's chief companion, though nowadays, in England, not many fishermen set off quite like that. Our legs are less active and the law is more so. Stephen Oliver had not to think of licenses for every fishing district, or of tickets from the local clubs, or of permissions from riparian owners jealous of their rights. If he saw a likely stream by the roadside he would set up his rod and cast a fly over it, and it never seems to have occurred to him that anybody might say him nay. Outside England there are countries where even today a wandering fisherman can do as Stephen Oliver did a hundred years ago. Did C—, P—, or I ask leave of anybody when, in a buckjumping Ford, we rattled and clattered to those Elysian rivers in the Livonian hills, slept in a peasant's barn, and, driven forth by fleas before the dawn and held from bed by fear of them at night, fished longer days than ever we have fished elsewhere? Good fishing it was, too, trout and grayling competed for only by a rare farmer with a 20-foot sapling and a fly that we called "The Young Sheep," a monstrous white woolly lump that did sometimes surprise us by rising a fish which thereupon left the water with great violence, flung clean overhead with the full force and sweep of a strong man wielding that tremendous engine. Unless there was a lot of water coming down, the fishers of "The Young Sheep" gave the river up to us as a bad job and were inclined to think that the success of the Wickhams and Bumbles that we foreign interlopers offered to their innocent and simple-minded fish was only to be explained by some private magic, a secret ointment, a charmed elixir, in which we dipped our flies. But it never occurred to them to question our rights. The wild fish were as the wild air, no man's possession but the free gift of God. That was ten years ago. There is a club now, but I doubt if it will make much difference. Its headquarters are a full day's journey away by country cart, and while it provides its members with chances of talking about fishing in town when all without is ice and snow, I do not suppose the fishers of "The Young Sheep" know much about it. If they know of it at all, it must amuse and puzzle them almost as much as did our tiny tinselled Wickhams.

But though such fishing is more and more seldom to be had for nothing, and though there is less and less temptation to copy Stephen Oliver and to tramp about a fishing district with no further preparation and equipment than a rod and tackle, a stout pair of legs and a volume by the contemporary Poet Laureate, fishing in general is coming to be more and more an affair of travel. Fishermen increase, and the number of those who are lucky enough to live on the banks of a river is very small in comparison with the number of those for whom the invariable prelude to fishing is a journey. Until quite recently its commonest prelude has been a journey by train. And it is of journeys by train that I find myself thinking while exulting, for the thousandth time, in the virtues of the fishing-rod as a travelling companion.

It may be that to think of railways in connection with going fishing is a sign of age. Perhaps I am celebrating something which is already in its last days (the stage coach had not many years left to it when Stephen Oliver discovered that its true purpose was to transport a man and a fishing-rod rapidly from London to the Yore). Perhaps, already, designers of motor-cars and aero-planes are spending days and nights in devising for the benefit of the fisher-man something as admirably suited to his purpose as the racks that have carried his rods so comfortably and for so long. A fishing-rod lying at full length in the rack of a railway carriage is safe against almost everything but malice. And there is not nearly so much malice about as a man is apt to be-lieve who is taking a new rod for its first journey. (Personally, I worry more about an old rod, but in either case it is unnecessary.) A hundred years of travelling by train with fishermen starting up nervously every time anyone puts a parcel on the rack that carries his travelling companion have taught the general public that a fishing-rod is as brittle as fine glass (which it is not). Be-sides, the jokes of many more than a hundred years have inclined them to humour us, to be kind to us while they smile, to indulge our foibles, and, in return for the amusement our mere existence offers them, to be gentle with our agate end-rings. Our fellow-passengers in motor-cars have still a lot to learn. If they see a fishing-rod so propped in a corner of a car as to be out of their way, their first instinct, always obeyed, is to grab it up, put it somewhere

G

else, and, in moving it, try to poke it through the roof. If we take rods with us in motor-cars, we take them at our own risk. But the change will come and may be close at hand. The fisherman's affection for his travelling companion is not a fickle fondness, to be lightly disregarded. Love will find out a way to the heart even of the motor manufacturer. Who knows, today or tomorrow, the sight of a strong man grieving over irreparable damage may move Mr. Ford or Mr. Morris to emulate the humanity of the railway engineer and to make journeys by motor-car at least not more dangerous for fishing-rods than they are for fishermen.

No man who has ever travelled with a fishing-rod finds himself able to travel happily without one. A rod marks the difference between travel and going to work, though, indeed, a rod in the rack is sometimes enough to make going to work a kind of holiday. It has a magic effect upon its owner, as he sits in the carriage beneath it, conscious of it. The sloth of the imagination is stirred by its mere presence. To have a rod in the rack over your head is to have the fishing faculties on the alert. The landscape swaying past the window is no meaningless phantasmagoria. The rivers are not sleeping beauties, but awake and beckoning as on a fishing day. The almost imperceptible gradients tell the traveller how he is passing from one watershed to another. Here is a little river that will join the Trent and so find its way to the Humber and the North Sea, and only a few miles further on is a streamlet hurrying towards the Mersey and the Dee. Here is a Yorkshire grayling stream and, before the lit pipe is ended, a stream with an altogether different rhythm working northward towards the Solway Firth. The presence of a rod in the rack above the traveller is enough to put mere land in its place, as something between rivers, as stepping-stones or viaducts, as material for river banks or beds. The water is the thing that matters. And, as the train, winding down a valley, meets a river again and again, the fisherman in his corner, all but fishing, sees the rise of a trout in the hang of a pool completed by another trout in another stretch of likely water.

A fishing-rod has its effect on others beside its owner. It has sometimes the virtues of the rod of Moses with which he struck the rock and water gushed out. The very sight of it will sometimes bring a spate of interesting talk from fellow-passengers who would otherwise have sat silent or quoted newspapers at each other. I remember a five-day journey across Europe, when, thanks to two rods in the rack, mine and another's, an argument started the first night, on the precise nature of the pleasure of fishing, and lasted till the journey's end, with such wealth of illustration, reminiscence, ingenious theory and counter-theory, as would have filled a tidy book. On this occasion one of the rods was a rod for bottom-fishing, so that the subject flew, from the very start, backwards and forwards, in one tremendous, sustained, and tireless rally, a shuttlecock between battledores, from float to fly, from fly to float, from "the contemplative man's recreation" to the sturdy upstream fishing in a fell beck that may leave a man six or seven miles from where he started, from the mystic concentration of the fisher for carp to the lusty ardours of the salmon-fisher, sitting on no wicker basket but, in his waders, leaning back against the current, cushioned, God-like, by the stream itself. Never, except when fishing, have I known time go so fast. There is, of course, the risk that the sight of a fishing-rod may provoke bores and the sort of person who quotes "The Angler's Prayer." But with such, even the mildest of fishermen has his ways of dealing.

Further, when he leaves the train, a fishing-rod does more for its fellow-traveller than any passport can do, no matter how magniloquent. It gives him a natural footing in a country and separates him instantly from those who are merely looking about them. The fisherman is no idle fellow. He brings his business with him. His rod serves the purpose of a barber's pole and proclaims its owner for what he is. He is recognised at once as a member of the guild, and without effort steps into his place. Between him and the Arab fishing within sight of the Pharos, on the very place, perhaps, where Cleopatra disgraced herself by playing that silly trick on fishing Antony, or the Egyptian crouched barefoot on the banks of Nile, or the Japanese intent on carp and poetry, is a close bond shared by none of those men with others of their own race who are not fishermen. Goldsmith travelled with a flute. Well, a flute is better than a camera or an opera glass. But a flute makes a man a little dependent on his neighbours. There will be times when they do not want to dance or even to listen. A fishing-rod, on the other hand, has all the social advantages of the flute, and at the same time makes no demands. Who better pleased than the fisherman if he have the river to himself? There he is, to be taken, as Stephen Oliver put it, "at his own intrinsic value." No one will wonder what he is up to. His waving rod, seen half a mile away, tells even those who are no fishermen that he has a part to play as old as man, almost. He may have come by train, on foot, by motor-car–no matter how. At least he has something to do besides gaping. He will be accepted from the first as a fellow-man and no tourist, a natural figure in the landscape and not an incomprehensible though happily fleecible off-comer.

These are the effects of a fishing-rod on others besides its owner. They should not be allowed to distract our attention from the manner in which it improves every journey on which it is a travelling companion. It takes, for example, fourteen days in the train to crawl home from Peking to Mukden, from Mukden to Harbin, up to the Manchurian frontier station, across Siberia, up, up, with slipping wheels to the top of the Urals, down, down, swaying, jolting and rattling, to the Volga, across the plains to Moscow, to Warsaw, to

Berlin, and so at last to some Dutch or Belgian port. But the fourteen days go fast if the ice has broken in the Siberian rivers, and the rod in the rack is promising fishing in England, and every bit of water crossed or passed makes that promise more emphatic and fishing more desperately desirable. There are the Chinese fishing in their canals, the Siberians anchored at the edges of their rapids, fishing over the sterns of their boats. There is the huge Lake Baikal (which has fish of its own unknown elsewhere), the Angara, the Yenisei, the Obi, and then the Volga and its tributaries that used to be fished by Aksakov (one of the most delightful of all writers on fishing, even if he did find fly-fishing "too restless") a hundred and thirty years ago. Then the Moscow river, with its memories of chub in August and those other great fish with so keen a taste for cockchafers, and the little fishing club which lost its boats in the first excitement of the Revolution but had them very properly restored when the fishermen represented that they ought to be considered as a co-operative society whose object it was to increase the food supply of the population. The last couple of days of that journey are hardly noticeable at all, so eagerly is the fisherman's mind casting ahead of him, and watching already for a rising trout in a pool nearly three hundred miles the other side of London.

But let no man envy distant journeys unless homeward bound. I doubt if it is ever worth while to make one for the sake of fishing. Fishing is one of the consolations of travel, not its proper object, for the best of all travelling with a rod is in one's own country. All foreign fishing is but makeshift after all, owing much of its pleasure to memories of home. The fish may be bigger, but what of that? The pride of catching a monster is shaded by the thought of how much greater that pride and that pleasure would have been if the big fish had been caught in home waters. These foreign leviathans do not count in the same way. They are somehow unreal. We may catch them and feel them tugging, but, abroad, we can hardly be said to be ourselves, and, as for the fish, at the bottom of our hearts we know them to be not much better than photographs, substitutes for English fish, with a flavour of artificiality about them, margarine instead of butter, more of them, perhaps, but not the same thing.

There is no need to urge a fisherman to carry his rod with him when he is on his way to the river, but, if I have learnt anything in the course of a life much of which has been spent in moving about, it is not to be without a rod in the rack even when the journey seems to be concerned with something else. Any rod is better than none; but the fly-rod is best of all. There distils from it a spiritual lightness, an unburdened glee that gives almost a dancing character to the thoughts of its owner, sedentary in his corner. The reasons for this are partly physical. The fly-rod needs so little circumstantial luggage. A matchbox, one of those excellent boxes sold with gramophone needles, a tooth-powder tin (this is excellently airtight), a flat cigarette tin (this fits comfortably

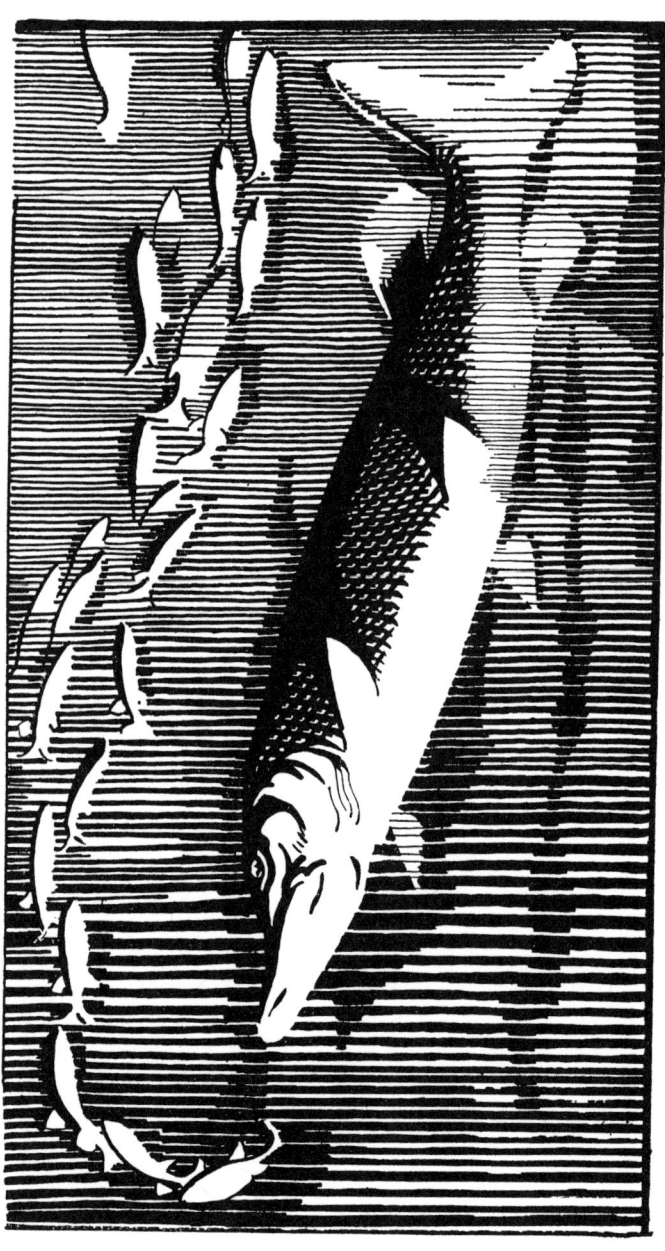

Plate V

in the pocket) or some other small receptacle for flies, or even a little covey of them perched on a patch of flannel inside the lapel of your coat, a reel, a cast or two to shame the business contents of your pocket-book, and you need no more to be free of the world's fishing. You know that with this slight equipment you can make something of any water anywhere. You can remind yourself that it is even an advantage to be without the landing-net or the gaff thought necessary by Mr. Oliver–for on the days when you have none, you catch, or at least hook, far bigger fish. You may never once, after seeing a river from a railway train, break your journey at the next station and go forth in your true character as a fisherman. But the knowledge that you could if you would is in itself something valuable and delightful.

Just as there is greater pleasure in tricking a fish with a feather and a bit of silk than in taking base advantage of his correct estimate of worm as worm, so the clean, delicate nature of the fly-fisher's instruments is reflected in his fastidious delights. It is not the fly-fisher of whom it must be said:

"Arm'd cap-a-pie with baskets, bags and rods,
The angler early to the river plods:
At night his looks the woeful truth announce,
The luggage half a ton, the fish . . . an ounce."

It *may* be said of him, it *has* been said of him, but it need not. He is not like the float-fisher, who must carry baits and ground-baits, sacks of bread and bran, bags of worms and maggots, a basket or a seat, floats, shot and plummets. No heaving of the lead for him. Nor yet is he like the spinner, who, also, has to carry things whose weight is part of their virtue. The fly-fisher deals in feathers and gossamer, and his luggage and his heart may be light together.

It may be objected that there are fish that will not take his fly and waters in which fly-fishing is impossible. There are not so many as are commonly believed. Almost all the so-called coarse fish are willing to die, if given the chance, in the manner usually reserved for their betters. Sturgeon are not. I believe they have to be foul-hooked, if hooked at all. But I have an old engraving which shows artificial flies intended to be used for carp. Kingsley's favourite fly for pike had a body "made of the remnants of the huntsman's new pink." The Duckling (a monstrous palmer of appropriate colour) is also a good fly for pike. So, they say, is a fly made of two peacock eye feathers set back to back. I have in my own box a well-tied specimen of a Mouse fly, bead-eyes and tail complete, meant to be fished dry. I should like to have caught a pike on a dry Mouse, and some day I will. But perhaps when you come to flies that copy birds and mammals you are approaching the borderline that separates fly- from bait-fishing. At the other end of the scale from pike are

[37]

minnows. In default of larger fish a man may do some very fine work with a
ooo midge on a minnow-haunted shallow. And somewhere between the pike
and the minnow come the chub. The last time I saw Sheringham, when I lay
ill and he, characteristically, came to offer to do my work for me as well as his
own, he was telling me of some time he had lately spent by a trout-stream
"but not wasting time on the trout . . . there were some chub in that place."
Everyone who knew him will know how almost as much by manner as by
word he made me see huge wary fish basking at the edge of deep green shadows, and, on the bank, an angler growing rather than moving in their direction, whereas, for that half-hour at least, trout turned into careless rowdy
commoners, hardly to be frightened off if a fisherman were to approach them
at a good round pace with a bow wave heralding his arrival.

That talk of fly-fishing for chub brought up a story of a stop at a frontier
station in Eastern Europe the officials of which are supposed by many to
spend their leisure in boiling their fellow-citizens alive, but do, in fact,
spend a great part of it fishing with worm and with bread paste in some water
that can be seen from the railway. The fisherman's rod passed their inspection without much difficulty. They had heard of such things, though they
used saplings themselves. Their suspicions were aroused by the reel. They
did not believe that the purpose of so elaborate an instrument could be what
they were told, and when, a moment later, the lid flew off a tooth-powder tin
and a cloud of laboriously tied flies scattered over the benches of the customs
house, they began to be convinced that here was something odd that ought to
be reported to headquarters. What were these things for? The same as the
reel, to catch fish. Impossible. Why, the feathers would get in the way of the
worms. Heads wagged more and more seriously, and the reel was unpacked
again and re-examined in the doubtful light of the flies. If the traveller were
lying to them on that subject, who could judge what deeper falsity might be
in him? There was a long wait at that station, and the fisherman offered to
demonstrate. He had seen something very like rises under some trees as the
train was coming in. Good. Three officials, two soldiers complete with rifles,
and one fisherman hurried across the lines to the little lake. The rod was put
up and a cast attached. With difficulty the officials and soldiery were persuaded to lie down instead of pressing to the water's edge. The rises were
those of rudd, which, though small, were sufficiently wise to move off as the
bank quivered under three pairs of official and two of military boots. But the
fisherman did his best, and in the end a small rudd put everything right by
fastening firmly on a tiny grayling fly (appropriately, a Red Tag). The fish,
with the fly in its mouth, was taken back to the station to prove the story true.
Half a dozen Red Tags were left, little feathered messengers of the true faith
in these remote parts, and the fisherman, freed from further troubles, was seen

[38]

off with military and official honour by the entire staff. Don't leave that story out, I was told.

So here it is with no more excuse than that it illustrates the kind of digression that is always possible to the man who takes with him a rod as travelling companion. And digressions, annoying as they are in a book, are usually the best part of a journey. Life itself, so they say, is a journey, and what would life be without fishing? The thought is unbearable, and so is a journey on which the traveller has left his fishing-rod behind.

CHAPTER V

by
Ferris Greenslet

THE FLY-ROD IN NORTH AMERICA

"The same old tremor of the Spring
Assails the heart of you and me;
Nor does the reel less blithely ring
By Willowemoc than by Dee."
JOHN BUCHAN: *To F. G.*

IT was the native American, the subtile Indian, who first cast a red hackle on the crinkled surface of an American trout-stream. It is recorded that the Indians of the Carolinas fished with a fly made from the skin of a buck's leg tanned with the hair on. This was wrapped around the shank of the hook with the hairs pointing away from the bend, and when drawn against the current must have bristled up, and moved itself aright in a most provocative manner. It was the tradition of the tribes that their fathers' fathers had taken fish in similar fashion. Their hook was of carved bone or hammered copper, the line of twisted fibre from the stems of the milkweed* or golden-rod, and it seems safe to suppose that the casting and killing implement was the indigenous cane or alder pole.

The white man was more backward in taking advantage of his opportunities. The contemporaries, even the friends, of Izaak Walton and Charles Cotton, who anchored in our estuaries in the seventeenth century selected town-

* Could this have been the "India weed" whose nature eluded Major Hills, author of the delightful and dependable *History of Fly Fishing for Trout?* My authority as to its use is the curator of the Indian Department of the Peabody Museum of Cambridge, Massachusetts, who states that lines made from it were hard, smooth, and of excellent strength.

sites because of the store of salmon found in adjacent pools, but left, so far as I can discover, no record of any immediate personal dealing with them. That seems to have been the affair of the retiaries.

On August 14, 1716, however, Cotton Mather recorded in his diary: "I rode abroad with some Gentlemen and Gentlewomen to take the Country Air, and to divert ourselves at a famous Fish pond. In the Canoe on the Pond, my foot slipt and I fell overboard into the Pond. Had the Vessel been a little further from the Shore, I must have been droun'd. But I soon recovered the Shore, and going speedily into a warm Bed I received no sensible Harm."

This misadventure was on Spy Pond in Cambridge, and the object of pursuit was presumably the yellow perch which still frequents its waters. Yet the action described rather suggests that the author of *Magnalia* was casting for a nobler quarry, rising in its beguiling way just beyond reach.

Old eighteenth-century battle maps of colonial wars, particularly those of New York and New England, contain many a meandering line labelled "trout brook"; and by the middle of the century evidences of angling for pleasure begin to multiply. *George Washington's Diaries* describe many days off from the labour of tobacco planting and horse breeding, days spent with the perch and catfish of the Potomac—not always, I regret to say, with rod and line. Certain other journals of the period kept in New York and New England enumerate good catches of substantial trout—if for the purposes of this paper I may so denominate *Salvelinus fontinalis*—some of them apparently with the fly. In the privately printed diary of John Rowe it is noted that in May, 1770, he took from the Mashpee River on Cape Cod several trout of 18 inches in length, the largest he had ever seen. Rowe, who was a prosperous Boston merchant and confirmed angler, had come from Exeter to the Bay Colony as a young man, bringing with him no doubt the type of fishing-rod recommended by Richard Bowlker's popular *Art of Angling*, a 14-footer of two pieces spliced together and fished without a reel.

After the Revolution, American fly-rods were either imported from England or imitated from British models. The specimens that have been preserved differ in no essential particular from the impressive lethal engines which adorn the walls of the Fly-Fishers' Club in Piccadilly. As a small boy, with an imagination already inflamed by angling literature and the capture of a few small bridge trout, it was my good fortune to inherit the equipment of an ancestor who caught his death by wading in a trout-stream on the first of May, which chanced to be at once the opening of the season and the eighty-fifth anniversary of his birth. There were creels and ivory-handled brass winches, several flasks of a good capacity, two books of flies of his own tying, chiefly grey hackles, and perhaps a half-dozen early Victorian rods. The *clou* of the collection was a 12-foot four-piece fly-rod of a really delightful soft whippiness.

The three lower joints were a dark mahogany hue–stained hickory, I imagine, or ash–while the top was of pale lemon-coloured lancewood. Casting it on a sunny day there was always to my young eyes an optical illusion by which the tip completely disappeared from view.

How vividly I remember working with it one day up the Old Maid's Brook, a tiny confluent of the Halfway Brook, a large stream then very much in spate. In the middle of the first meadow a 6-inch ribbon of black water slid through a bed of cowslips. One of the grey hackles was dapped into this watery crack. A terrific subaqueous explosion, and fourteen muscular inches of silver, red, and gold were deposited as with a derrick amid the cowslips. But the rod, alas! had become a five-piece rod; and it was never repaired.

Another item of my inheritance was a "Sunday rod," a telescopic construction of whole cane, ornamented with bands of red and green. It appeared quite virgin of any use, and I suspect my ancestor, a known follower of Tom Paine, instead of employing it as a walking-stick on Sunday mornings, trudged off quite brazenly to the stream side, marching to the rhythm of church bells with twelve feet of hickory over his shoulder.

It was in the blood. An ancestor of his had come to the colonies in 1759 as an aide to Amherst, sent to avenge Montcalm's defeat of Abercrombie and capture Ticonderoga. As the scarlet-coated army of 13,000 men moved north through the pine woods, along a trail cut 10 rods wide to avoid surprise, this aide was left in command of a blockhouse on the Halfway Brook, already mentioned, so called because it bisected the 16-mile march from Fort Edward on the Hudson to Fort William Henry on Lake George. When Ticonderoga had fallen and the war was over, the trouting in the brook had proved so satisfactory that the commandant of the blockhouse decided to remain where he was, and divided the remainder of a long life, so family tradition says, between agriculture and halieutics. On the site of his little fishing fortress stands a marker of bronze and granite. I like to think it is a monument to the 2-pounders which he, as a poet of his own time puts it, did with yielding rod solicit to the shore.

It is in the blood still. One afternoon on the Tay at Dunkeld the kelts were willing but the fish were dour. To while away the slack hours we entered a half-ruined abbey on the river bank and fell almost at once on a tablet to the officers of the Black Watch killed at Ticonderoga. Queer, ancestral, questioning thrill! Did one's double great-grandsire experience a peculiar poignancy in his fishing pleasures from the thought of comrades facing musket and tomahawk just a little beyond? Certainly oneself had known a profound half shamefaced satisfaction during a week on the Barle in the cheerless March of 1917. And is there not an intensity in Walton's passion for the tranquillity of smooth flowing waters, that was engendered from the civil wars?

[45]

It was during another and bloodier Civil War, that between the States, that the one great epoch-making development in the fly-rod took place. Some few years before the stage coach had yielded forever right of way to the railway carriage, and the three-piece fishing-rod which could now be carried without prodding one's neighbour had superseded the four-jointed weapon. In England rods made of three and four strips of cane split longitudinally, glued, and whipped together, had begun to compete with the recently introduced greenheart—not very successfully at first, though as a material for tops the invention had its admirers. The rod as a whole was expensive and not satisfactory.

About 1850, the very year in which at least three makes of four-strip split-bamboo fly-rods were shown at the Royal Exhibition,* one Samuel Philips, who made rifles and fowling-pieces in Easton, Pennsylvania, began to experiment with fishing-rods of split cane. No doubt the proximity of that admirable river the Brodhead suggested a profitable side line. At any rate, after trying three- and four-strip construction, he hit upon the Big Idea and produced the first six-section hexagonal rod, now standard the world over.

By the time the first gun was fired on Fort Sumter these were being produced commercially by one Murphy, who may have learned his craft by the banks of the Lee or the Shannon, and were sold by Andrew Clerk and Company, of New York. It was, however, the greater pains and superior craftsmanship of Hiram L. Leonard that first gave the hexagonal split bamboo its undisputed pre-eminence. Leonard made his first rods towards the end of the Civil War in Bangor, Maine, doorway to a thousand lakes and connecting streams holding trout. Finding, however, that his best market was among the prosperous fishermen of New York, he moved to Central Valley in Orange County of that State, close to the classic waters of the Beaverkill, Neversink, and Willowemoc; went into partnership with Thomas B. Mills, and set up the factory which still continues to operate. By 1875 the words "Leonard rod" were synonymous with the best in bamboo. In the early eighties Mr. F. E. Thomas went from Bangor to Central Valley to become Leonard's foreman, but returned to Maine a decade later to set up for himself. Hiram Leonard died some fifteen years ago, and it is fair to say that there is a double apostolic succession, a dual laying on of practised hands, whereby both the present shops of Thomas and Leonard carry forward the gospel of rod-making according to Hiram. Neither are, as things go, large enterprises, but though there is a rod and tackle manufactory in the middle west that boasts an annual

* In the same year, I am informed, Charles F. Orvis, of Manchester, Vermont, on the Battenhill, first omitted dowels from male ferrules, and originated the suction joint. He also devised what I believe to have been the first perforated and contracted reel. He was a sound writer on angling topics, and his daughter Elizabeth Orvis Marbury was the author of the compendious *Favourite Flies and their History*.

"turnover" of some 2,000,000 dollars, there is no real competition with the products of Bangor and Central Valley.

Most experienced American anglers turn to English tacklists for reels and lines, casts, waders, fishing bags, nets, flies, priests and other gadgets, but I think we feel that for whatever reason, perhaps because cane seasons more completely in a dry than in a humid climate, the native American hexagonal split bamboo is a better rod to fish with than the beautifully finished and seductive merchandise of St. James's and Pall Mall. I have succumbed to the charms of no less than four London rods, and shall doubtless do so again. I give them each an occasional airing, usually by lending them to ladies; but on the stream, particularly over heavy fish in broken water, there is a brisk and eager resiliency in my three Thomases that is not only a delight, but an inspiration and an example to the fisherman. To each of the three I have given a name from angling history: Izaak, Sir Henry, and Juliana. I would like to chronicle their memorable victories: Izaak's 72 fish of $1\frac{1}{2}$ pounds or better in six days from Misere Stream; Sir Henry's 5-pounder to the Iron Blue on Rapid River; Juliana's brace of 14-inchers from the Funshion, under the ruined walls of Glanworth, what time I, in a dinner jacket, having eaten and drunk deep of Irish hospitality, essayed to show a salmon-fisher from home, who had never seen it done, how a trout was taken on a floating fly. A bad mess I made of it, too, until dinner wore off; but Juliana saw me through, and finally, between 11 and 11.15 p.m., the double kill was put through. All three of these favourite rods, be it noted, are 9-footers, except Sir Henry. He started life at 9 feet 6 inches, but has lost 3 inches in active service and is the better for it.

A few weeks ago there appeared in the London *Times* a review of two recent fishing books, entitled "American Trout Fishing." I quote the central paragraph:

"The fly used by the angler is apparently neither in fact nor conception a copy of any particular species, while the method pursued, with dry as much as with wet fly, is admittedly 'chuck and chance it.' From this circumstance, paradoxically, arises the only improvement which our American pupils have been able to contribute–the use of exceptionally light rods, which, though increasingly in vogue, are a mere luxury on the British chalk-stream where the actual casting is intermittent, whereas to the American, fishing continuously and making in addition the necessary false casts to dry his fly, the labour of using any but the lightest available rod is almost prohibitive."

While it is true that among imitators of Cotton Mather, who fish in ponds from canoes, there has been a great acclaim over the fairy rod of 7 or 8 feet, weighing 2 or 3 ounces or less, I think there is now among stream fishermen a very definite reaction toward heavier timber, and precisely for the opposite reason to that stated. It is the labour of casting with the overlight rod that is prohibitive. One is continually forcing it and is wearied by its constant inadequacy. It is as if one were to play a round of golf, carrying no club heavier than a light mashie. A truly resilient rod of 9 or 9½ feet, weighing five honest ounces, does the work for you; and when the big moment comes, and the 4-pounder starts to go where it were better that he should not go, you have command of the situation.

Nor can it be admitted that we tie our flies without an eye on the natural object, and chuck them and chance it. It is, alas! only too true that our comparatively weedless streams produce but a scattering and a meagre hatch compared to the moving lunch counter which is offered twice daily to pampered British trout. Yet it is decidedly an off day on a good river in May or June when duns of great variety, or some of the sedges, are not in evidence with fish moving to them. The point is that the hatch being scattering and unsatisfactory, the trout who would get a square meal off the ephemeridæ, who prefers them, perhaps, to caddis and grubs, must be on the alert through a much longer portion of the day than suffices his cousin *Fario* in the old country. Neither does he wait till the table is all spread before setting to, but is ready to take the first individual fly, even a well delivered imitation, that comes over him.

Yes, "imitation." We have for the most part, after gazing upwards through various contrivances at flies floating on the water against the background of the sky, left off the wings that, when well cocked, are a delight to the fisherman's eye, whatever they may look like to the fish's. Our *mimesis* is the visual realism of Velasquez and Vermeer, not the near-sighted actuality of the painted dollar bill. The little badger-hackled flies which most of us affect, tied with bodies of the proper colour and value, due consideration being given to the transparency, translucency, or opacity of the same, are, if not meticulously correct imitations of any of God's trout-stream creatures, at any rate, compelling suggestions. I have done well with them on fairly difficult water in England and Ireland, and heavy fish are reported to have been taken by them from the Kennet and the Test.

As for chucking them and chancing it, the man who does that will come home with a bag as deflated as he went out withal. Either his flies will float over fishless eddies, or he will line his quarry before the fly swims into its ken. We have had perforce to make a study of fish positions; of the kind of rock a fish will harbour by and the kind that he will not; of the major and minor foci of mingled currents or braided ribbons of water where the food converges and good fish are most often found. In process of time experience crystallises into a kind of instinct of second nature. I have seen a good dry fly man fish up a stretch of broken water with no fish showing, not casting continually but

Plate VI

selectively, significantly, perhaps once in every 20 or 30 yards, and take or raise a fish at nearly every cast; though it is fair to say that he had fished the water before.

Casting to feeding fish, putting the fly just above where that spreading ring or single large bubble made its gratifying appearance, is unquestionably the more luscious form of the sport. I think it is also the easier, though not in memory the more rewarding. The rising trout has advertised to the world his exact location, that he is hungry and ready to do business. He has even indicated the precise article of diet he at the moment prefers. In the case of the non-rising fish you have both discovered and compelled him. There is an element of miracle in the episode which is not the least of its charms.

Personally I must confess that upstream nymphing *à la* Skues seems the most perfectly delightful of all methods of inveigling trout. In July, 1919, fresh from the belated reading of *Minor Tactics*, I encountered below a dam on the Callicoon a brace of good brown trout obviously bulging; nothing floating interested them in the slightest. After a hurried mental consultation with myself, I made an impromptu nymph by cutting the wings and hackle from a dry Wickham, leaving only the lucent whiskery body. This makeshift was attached to a dry leader with a wet point, and presently both the bulgers becomingly wrapped up together in a blue bandana handkerchief were in the bag. Thereafter I have seldom missed, and often made, an opportunity to practise the minor tactic. Ten years later came an invitation from the author of *Fishing Ways and Wiles*, the expert practitioner of many, to fish his water on the Tees, over the Easter holidays. The bystanders at the club where the invitation was delivered assured me that Tees trout could be taken only by a secret method known to their proprietor alone, and that any efforts of mine would infallibly prove futile. On that enchanting river, however, it was disclosed that the famous secret method was nothing more or less than my old pursuit of upstream nymphing. I did not, I hope, make the complete ass of myself that had been so freely predicted.

Though I have taken leave to differ from the writer in *The Times* in regard to some details of the fly-rod in America and its use, I am sure that American fishermen are profoundly and forever grateful to the English colleagues whose sharp eyes, logical minds, and skilful hands have given us both the minor and the major tactics which we have adapted to our rougher usage.

We have, nevertheless, been following the preferred methods tentatively and haphazardly longer than is generally supposed. No anthology of early references to the floating imitation should omit Thaddeus Norris, a rodmaker and fly-tier of Philadelphia, whose *American Angler's Book* was published in 1864. Norris had apparently been reading Stewart's *The Practical Angler*, published seven years earlier, and experienced an uneasy sense of conviction of sin in fishing down stream. He confesses that although he has tried to fish up, he doubts the possibility of the practice in our swift-running rivers, since the fly came back at him so fast that it was continually afoul of his pantaloons. But listen to him on the floating fly:

"If it could be accomplished, the great desideratum would be to keep the line wet and the flies dry. I have seen anglers succeed so well in their efforts to do this by whipping the moisture from their flies, that the stretcher and dropper would fall so lightly, and remain so long on the surface, that a fish would rise and deliberately take the fly before it sank.

"One instance of this kind is fresh in my memory: it occurred at a pool beneath the fall of a dam on the Willowemoc, at a low stage of water—none running over. The fish were shy and refused every fly I offered them, when my friend put on a Grannom for a stretcher, and a minute Jenny Spinner for a dropper. His leader was of the finest gut and his flies fresh, and by cracking the moisture from them between each throw, he would lay them so lightly on the glassy surface, that a brace of trout would take them at almost every cast, and before they sank or were drawn away. He had tied these flies and made his whip especially for his evening cast on this pool, and as the fish would not notice mine, I was obliged to content myself with landing his fish, which in a half-hour counted several dozen. Here was an exemplification of the advantage of keeping one's flies dry."

Surely Thaddeus was *anima naturaliter christiana*! Yet he was a long way in advance of his time. H. P. Wells, writing twenty years later, and a most inquiring and multifarious fly-fisherman, mentions no fly copied from any natural insect, and never even suggests that trout ever feed on such things. He fished chiefly in ponds in the wilderness where the trout and landlocked salmon are predominantly bottom feeders. There to this day the most killing fly is his own Parmachenee Belle, a confection of scarlet, white, and yellow, and a correct imitation of the ventral fin of a small trout. Is the great trout the victim of a fin fetich?

Any comparison between fishing in England and in the United States must recognise as its basis the vast superiority of England in the number of rivers containing trout, and the density of the trout population in them. For the purposes of the fly-fisherman, New York State, Pennsylvania, and New England constitute a geographical unit exceeding in area the entire British Isles. Yet the streams in this area worth his serious attention can be reckoned in dozens, whereas in the *British Angler's Diary* and *Where to Fish* streams supplying fair trouting are listed, literally, by the hundred. The disparity in density is even greater. I have stood on the bridge in front of the Swan Inn at Bibury on the Coln and thrown a handful of bread crumbs on the water. Instantly thirty or forty solid fish came on the feed. Save in certain northern streams in September where fish from large lakes congregate in anticipation of their amours, I know no pool on any river in this country where such a sight would be seen; and I think it is typical, not exceptional. Here if we find one fish to a pool we are happy; if a brace, it is a thing to tell about.

On a few rivers that have been heavily and continuously stocked, the population may be a little denser than this, but going from the very best of our streams to a second-class English or Irish river, the angler's first impression is of the extraordinary number of fish in evidence. He doesn't bring many more to the net than he would at home, but it is a surprising comfort to him to feel that so many are there. Here they come and go. Last year, perhaps, owing to some unusual political activity on the part of the fishculturists of a state there may have been really good, dependable fishing in a certain river. Next year you may motor 500 miles and spend a week wading its rocky runs and never see a fish. Save in the ponds and connecting thoroughfares of the great north woods a large *Fontinalis* is fast becoming as legendary as the caribou. Millions of lively fingerlings are annually put by the state hatcheries into waters that have become unsuitable for them. Only a very few survive to become respectable ½-pounders and make glad some fly-fisherman's heart.

It is to the brown and rainbow trout that we shall have to look for the solace of our old age. They thrive in water of a temperature that turns the *Fontinalis* belly up, and with sufficient feed reach the 2-pound estate within three years. A 10-inch native trout in the same water may be ten years old. Best of all, they are free risers, and sporting fish after connection is established. The play of each of the three species is characteristic: the *Fontinalis* for plunging strength, the rainbow for dash and speed, the brown for stubborn, recalcitrant wiliness! A rainbow hooked 30 feet up stream is down between your legs and leaping high in the air 40 feet below before you can say "priest." *I have seen this happen*, and had to assist the dazed fisherman to lift his brogue over the line! The brown trout, on the other hand, has a genius for knowing the exact location of the principal snags in the pool and making his way thither with all but irresistible determination. When he surrenders, he surrenders handsomely. He is a stout-hearted gentleman, and, in his way, a scholar.

Persistent stocking of brown trout with a sprinkling of rainbows is, I repeat, our best hope for the future, provided it can be coupled with a large size and a small bag limit. Surely a trout should be 10 inches long, in some waters 12, before he is taken away from his parents, and two, or at the most three, brace of these ought to satisfy any reasonable appetite for trout meat. More and more fishermen, on heavily fished water, are coming to play an amusing game with the trout. If he gets in the net he loses, and you score one; but no more than in golf or dominoes is it necessary that you should put the priest to your vanquished opponent and eat him. It is better that he should live to lose again another day.

In compensation for our inadequacies in the matter of *salmonidæ* the River Gods have provided us with another game fish, the small-mouthed black bass, who will put the stoutest fly-rod through all its paces. A free riser at certain times of the year, a strong and varied fighter, the holder of the international record in the high jump, he is in the fullest sense a sporting fish. Personally however, I must confess to a lack of perfect sympathy with him. Though he takes your Silver Doctor with *élan*, you know in your heart he would rather have a frog, a crayfish, or the unspeakable helgramite. His favourite morsel of them all seems to be the "bass plug." This is usually a highly painted affair of wood and aluminium with little spinning propeller-like objects attached. When under way it looks like nothing in the world so much as a small submarine running awash. Furthermore, the waters he inhabits possess as a rule less of beauty for the eye and soothing for the spirit than the meadow or mountain streams where the trout and salmon dwell. He lacks the enchantment of association–of literature.

Other fish, too, can give the American fly-rod its needed exercise. A friend of mine, the most knowledgeable dry fly man of my acquaintance, an accurate entomologist, a subtle tier of floating flies, with that craft of the hand and eye which has made so many good painters good fishermen, amuses himself in off hours by seeing how long a list of different fishes he can take with a fly. Perhaps it would be more precise to say with feathers, for his devices for the special undoing of some new variety bear faint resemblance to anything that flies with wings. Here is his list of conquests to date:

Fresh Water	*Salt Water*
Trout	Mackerel
Salmon	Pollock
Yellow Perch	Blue Fish
White Perch	Striped Bass
Black Bass	Herring
Rock or Calico Bass	Flounder
Wall-eyed Pike	Codfish
Pickerel	
Sun Fish	
Dace	

I believe he aspires to catfish and shark.

Perhaps the most distressing present difference between fishing in America and in the British Isles lies in the important business of quenching thirst. Anglers have always been connoisseurs in that matter, and one of our presidents has said that the mark of the true fisherman is that he draweth not his flask in secret. But consider the sorry case of the American today. His British brother takes a bottle of claret to the stream side, if, as the old fishing book says, "he has a boy to carry it." Failing the boy and the claret, he has only to fish along up to the bridge, where there is sure to be an inn and a mug of bitter to restore him. When the evening rise is over, and the last 2-pounder has broken him darkly in the weeds, he returns to a late dinner mitigated by Bristol cream, Rhine wine, more claret, and burgundy, with a glass of port or old brandy after. Then when the events of the day have been fully discussed and proper lessons derived from them, he retires to his virtuous slumbers, warmed, if the evening be chilly, by a noggin of hot Scotch or rum.

Here in this day of wrath our chief recourse for courage or consolation, even when we have gone over our waders, or lost Leviathan, is gin–gin of our own making, aged during the time consumed in its transfer from the demijohn to the shaker. But we must not complain too loudly. Home-made gin mingled with barbless vermouth is really not so bad; and there are the documents to prove that the juice of the juniper is the traditional drink of the American angler. Listen again to Thaddeus Norris. He describes in 1864 his preparations for a trip to Colebrook, then as now a well-known fishing station on the Connecticut River:

"There were three of us: our baggage as follows–Item, one bottle of gin, two shirts: Item, one bottle schnapps, two pair stockings: Item, one bottle Schiedam, one pair of fishing-pants: Item, one bottle genuine aromatic, by Udolpho Wolfe, name on the wrapper, without which the article is fictitious, one pair extra boots: Item, one bottle extract of juniper-berry; one bottle brandy, long and wide, prescribed by scientific skill for medicinal purposes. Also, rods, tackle in abundance, and a supply of gin; in addition, each of us had a quart-flask in our pockets, containing gin. We also had some gin inside when we started."

No wonder he didn't like to fish up stream!

From all of this it appears that the use of the fly-rod in America tends, unless we take heed, to become something of a hectic pursuit rather than that peaceful recreation specially recommended for the Contemplative Man. Trout are few and far off. We begin the campaign by driving at a furious pace for some hundred of miles along a crowded concrete highway. Once on the stream it is usually necessary to cover a league of water to produce fair results. The spirit of the "go-getter" invades us, and we actually indulge in a foot race with the local sportsman, equipped with a telescopic steel rod and large night-walking worms, who knows even better than we do just where the biggest fish lie. How different from the water meadows of England where, after a leisurely breakfast, one strolls out with rod and pipe, confident that one has but to choose a position, consolidate it, and take one's ease; the trout in their own good time will come to one. There fishing with the fly is what it should be—not so much a competitive sport as a branch of philosophy.

But I fancy the mood of the actual fishing is the same everywhere. It is always, I think, a restrained and muted fierceness. It is in the casting of the fly, when a moment's languor is fatal; in the striking and playing of the fish. It is the source of numberless acts of unrecorded heroism, as when rheumatic old men deliberately go over their waders to cover a rising fish without drag. It is a fire in the heart that drives us on to one more pool long after we are thoroughly exhausted and reprehensibly late for dinner. The Indians knew it, as they cast their buck tails on virgin waters, and my ancestor, God rest him, felt its propelling urge on his eighty-fifth birthday. In short, it is fishing.

And of fishing the fly-rod is the characteristic implement and perfect symbol. How its yielding resiliency typifies the character of the great men who have graced its annals, and of many a mute inglorious fisherman, too! What magical comfort comes to us on winter nights, when the world and its unreason have been too much with us, from the mere handling of its shining strength! When spring is not far behind and trout begin to cast an upward eye, and city-pent fishermen make strange passes with their walking-sticks, it is my habit to set a bundle of three or four rods and a net handle or two in some conspicuous position where the eye will fall frequently on it. That precious roll is the emblem of a gentler fascism than the Italians have represented by their bundle of stolid staves. It stands for direct action presently to come, for golden memories of vanished days, and for enduring friendship with kindred minds, companions along the rivers of home and by streams beyond the estranging sea.

CHAPTER VI

by
Knut Dahl

FLY-FISHING IN NORWAY

WHEN conforming to the wish of my friend Mr. Sheringham by writing a few words on the fly-rod in Norway, I am to some extent at a loss how to begin. The subject has so many sides. Some of them are purely sentimental, some utilitarian and commercial, while some of them are historical. Indeed, when revolving the subject, it presents itself almost faceted, reflecting innumerable aspects of human life and human nature.

Why does man fish with the rod? An answer in detail would surely be a very composite thing. But most of us, I think, would answer truly if we said that we fished because we must. Without commenting upon the fact, we might give our answer in the plain words of a forest labourer of my juvenile acquaintance. He was frequently neglecting his work in order to satisfy his craving for the noble art of angling. His only excuse was: "When I get the angling fit, I must angle." No comments. Only the short, almost inarticulate statement of the operation of a law of nature. This primitive man had no power of expression, no vocabulary descriptive of the joy which pervaded his soul when he relinquished the tedium of his toil for the delight of the forest tarn, the breezy lake, or the dark pools of the river. He could not describe the elation he knew, the sense of freedom, the harmonious effects of the beautiful landscape, the soothing stillness of the lily-covered tarn, the fierce and entirely disproportionate delight of flinging the luckless perch sky-high and breaking their quivering necks. Nor could he describe or decipher the primitive element in his savage joy, when in his miserable bark humpy he fried and ate the perch, and after a night's sleep on a bed of pine boughs he resumed his toil with the logs. But it was all there in his simple words.

And very few of us could describe why we fish, because it is a primitive thing. However civilised, however sophisticated and tied down by duties and

K

conventions and considerations we are, in all of us, brethren of the fly-rod, there is a primitive element, a remnant of the savage, a craving for the delights of nature. And when we yield to this primitive urge the freedom of the savage becomes ours. The fly-rod becomes the magic wand, at whose touch the gates open into a world below the surface of the civilised community, hidden in the landscapes, limited only by the waters of this globe. The charm of the sport is not so much what we may achieve, but the spirit in which we achieve it, and what we may find in this world below the surfaces. Our own illusions add a charm to what otherwise is commonplace, a beauty to things and localities which others do not see. Even the most distant wilderness, the loneliness and discomfort of which makes it abhorrent to refined man, becomes the paradise where our most primitive desires are fulfilled, because it is in harmony with the primeval elements of our nature.

Even if our own powers of illusion may extract pleasures from the waters of civilised or even heavily farmed lands, still the virgin waters of the wilderness are the object of our dreams.

Not so very long ago one might say that Norway, broadly speaking, was a virgin country from a fisherman's point of view. Until the beginning of the nineteenth century fly-fishing, or fishing as a sport, was an unknown thing, and at that time only a very few gentlemen who had been subject to English influence patronised the sport.

The early inauguration of the sport of fly-fishing in Norway was thus without doubt of British origin, and most of its early development was due to the same source.

Thus in the first two or three decades of the nineteenth century an increasing number of English travellers went to Norway mainly for the purpose of salmon fishing. Norway was in those days an out-of-the-way country, accessible only in private yachts or occasional sailing vessels, and to go to Norway was at that time quite an expedition into a distant and little known land, which to the early pioneers must have presented a striking and unusual charm. Not only did it offer scenery of great beauty, and a simple, honest, and hospitable population, but the salmon fishing was exceedingly good, because the commercial fishing was as yet in a very primitive and undeveloped state.

At that time nearly all commercial fishing was done in the rivers. The farmers fished for their own use and for markets more or less local, which could absorb preserved–pickled or smoked–products of salmon. The early sportsmen got permission to fish either free or for an almost nominal fee, the farmers obtaining the fish and being pleased at getting somebody to do their fishing for nothing. There was then no fishing in the sea worth mentioning, only comparatively few old-fashioned fixed engines being employed. Almost all the salmon were allowed to enter the rivers, which, however, from time immemorial had been full of traps and other fixed engines for the purpose of capturing salmon.

It is, to my mind, doubtful whether the stock of salmon in those days was virtually larger than at the present time, because the gross mismanagement of the river fishing at that time probably left a very small stock of spawning fish. But there is no doubt that the proportion of the salmon stock that entered the rivers was comparatively much larger.

If the sportsman found the old traps and engines in the way of his sport he could, as a rule, arrange to buy them off and thus have the run of splendid fishings. These conditions gradually took a larger and larger number of British sportsmen to the Norwegian rivers, most of which were fished by Englishmen as early as between 1830 and 1840.

Later on the development of the commercial salmon fisheries began, and from the sixties the competition from the netsmen on the coast made itself more and more felt, an increasing proportion of the salmon being captured before they could reach the rivers.

During this period, however, a government inspector of salmon fisheries was appointed, and the salmon fisheries of Norway were for the first time subjected to proper supervision and legislation, which gradually did away with much of the old mismanagement. A great development ensued, and from the seventies and towards the end of the last century the Norwegian salmon fisheries enjoyed a very prosperous period, the net fishings in the sea steadily increasing in value, and the rivers also doing well. It appeared possible to keep a fair balance between the commercial fishing and the rod fishing in the rivers without materially diminishing the stock of fish. In these endeavours the letting of the rivers for sport was a great help, as the old and sometimes very noxious engines in the rivers were bought off and the rods left a proportionately large stock for spawning.

The sea nets, however, developed so much in number that at the end of the century there were upwards of 8,000 of them, and it appeared as if the toll they took of the stock of salmon would in the long run be too heavy. A considerable drop in the yield of Norway's salmon fisheries in the first and second decades of the present century appeared to favour this opinion. As a consequence of this decrease, however, the number of nets was constantly reduced towards 1914. During the War their number also went down, until in 1918 there were only about 5,000 nets. The yield of the fisheries again rose appreciably, and the bag-nets again increased in number, so that during the last few years their numbers have once more risen until they now equal the figures for the beginning of the century.

Now the old apprehensions are beginning to reassert themselves, and these find support in a decreasing yield and a disproportion between the outcome from net and rod fishings. Many of the rivers have given disappointing results, a fact which, however, does not only apply to Norwegian rivers, but is shared also by British rivers, which for the last two seasons have been exceedingly disappointing.

I shall not here enter upon a detailed discussion of the possibilities of the improvement of the present state of fishings in Norway. The proper balancing of sea nettings *versus* rod fishings is one of the most difficult problems in the supervision of Norwegian salmon fisheries. But our new law governing these should probably do some good by the restrictions it puts on the nets. Another fact is also important. The whole organisation of the rod fishings in Norway, the lettings and sub-lettings of the beats, and also the prices for such fishings, were severely jolted during and after the War, and we still suffer from the after-effects. In time things will get better.

But one thing is certain: the wonderful and virgin fishings which fell to the lot of the early salmon fishermen, when all the fish ran up the rivers unhampered by nets in the sea–these will never fall to any man's lot again. Once invented and used, the sea nets will stay. Their use may be to some extent restricted in the interest of the stock, their numbers may go down in periods of scarcity, but the sportsman will always have to reckon with more or less competition from them, just as he has had to do for the last fifty years or more.

And he must also remember another fact. In the old days the British angler had all Norway's salmon fishings to himself. He was a dear and well-liked guest. He was a feature in every valley. The arrival of the "Engelsmann" was just as steadfast a phenomenon as the arrival of the migratory birds, who came from southern lands to stay for our short northern summer. And he brought with him notions, customs, and suggestions, strange to begin with, but he left them behind, and a friendship and understanding between the two nations sprang from these relics. And there is also one thing–he taught us of Norway how to fish for salmon, and the English angler of the present day has to count on an increasing number of Norwegian competitors of his own making. But we like our English brother, and Norway is a large country which has 160 salmon rivers where a modest angler may still get a salmon or two.

While the rod fishing for salmon in Norway is entirely of British origin, and has also been developed largely by Britishers, the same does not quite apply to fly-fishing for trout, char and other fish.

To be sure, the rods, the technique, the ideas first came from Britain, but the development of the sport of fly-fishing for trout and other fish in Norway has been mainly due to the Norwegians themselves. Being poor, most of us could not afford salmon fishings, and our fishing was done in the domain of the trout and other fish.

[60]

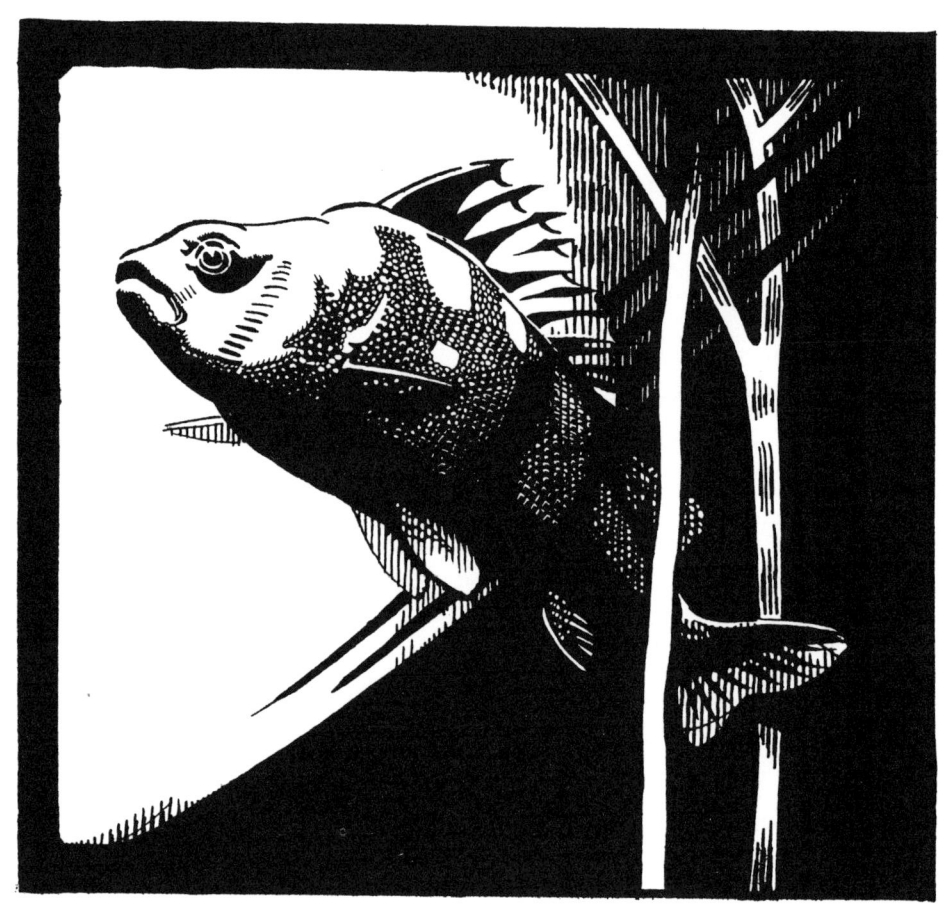

Plate VII

Just as the adventurer into Norwegian salmon fishing a hundred years ago did not have far to go, so the pioneer trout fishermen of Norway found virgin grounds close at hand.

Thus our great folklorist P. C. Asbjørnsen, living in Oslo about the middle of last century, would take his rod out and in the course of an evening's stroll in the neighbourhood of the town enjoy a bag of fair trout, and in almost every river and lake the traveller bent on fishing could usually be sure of excellent sport. Certainly the conditions in the Norway of those days were far from what one could call pristine. The local inhabitants had from time immemorial fished its waters more or less rationally—sometimes rather less rationally. But, broadly speaking, the country was, at least from the fly-fisher's point of view, virgin. And this virginity lasted far into the century. For one thing, the followers of the fly-rod were for a long time comparatively few, and the means of travel were limited and difficult. Until after the sixties railways were very few, and the far-off valleys and mountain regions which were the real strongholds of trout could only be reached by long and laborious travels by carriage, or finally by tramping it into remote places where housing and food were either primitive, or where the adventurer had to rough it and fend for himself as well as he could.

The writings of some of these pioneer fishermen bear testimony to the delightful reward awaiting those who took their rods into such distant places. British and Norwegian sporting literature presents enough instances of this fact, and we may as an example mention the delightful books of Professor Friis and the world-renowned British book *Three in Norway*, than which latter no more delightful book has been written on fly-fishing in our country.

But even in places not remote from civilisation conditions often continued to be very favourable for a long time.

Even I, who began fishing in the early eighties, contemporaneous with *Three in Norway*, can remember the fishing at my native place as very good. My home was situated only 20 miles from Oslo, but our only means of communication was a road rarely travelled by others than the inhabitants of the valley. The river teemed with trout and grayling, and although the fishing was free it sufficed for everybody in the valley. These conditions remained practically the same, and the fishing continued to be good, until a railway was built in the last years of last century. During the construction of the railway the irrepressible navvy—who in Norway is always a fierce fisherman—fished for all he was worth, and after the railway began to run an influx of "alien" fishermen from Oslo in a few years ruined the fishing.

What happened in that valley is to some extent illustrative of what has happened to the trout fishings of Norway.

Up to the end of last century the tourist could travel along the main tourist roads up the main valleys–the Setesdal, the Telemarken, the Numedal, Hallingdal, Valdres, Gudbrandsdal–and he would find fairly good hotel accommodation along these lines, and fairly good fishing in the vicinity of the hotels; and venturing a little off these roads, he would generally meet with grand fishing.

But after that time a number of railways, right through the country, have been completed. The Bergen, the Valdres, the Romsdal, the Dovre railways have been constructed and have opened up to the ever-increasing number of Norwegian fishing enthusiasts the charms and possibilities of enormous tracts of lake and river, which formerly were only accessible to few people. Add to this the greatly increased facilities for motor transport, and it will be easily understood that there are excellent reasons for the decrease in fish and the deterioration of the sport, which makes itself felt in many of the old fly-fishing resorts.

The Norwegians being very keen sportsmen and the passion for fly-fishing being common to all classes, the accessible localities are in many places apt to be overfished. And the development has been so sudden, and the new conditions are of so recent a date, that the proper remedies have not yet been found, although there is a great movement tending to improve the fishings and to bring them under better management. But, as it is, the traveller intent on fly-fishing will look in vain for the old and idyllic conditions which used to prevail along the tourist routes twenty to thirty years ago. He will in some places –where waters have been preserved or subjected to a reasonable management– find good or even excellent fishings close to hotels and tourist resorts. But these are rather the exception than the rule; usually he must go further afield. Nevertheless, Norway is a large country, and it has more than 200,000 lakes and tarns, and innumerable rivers which all hold trout or other sporting fish. Very few of them are now virgin; but a great many of them are remote and rarely fished and will open their charms to the adventurous fisherman.

Broadly speaking, we may review the chances meeting a fisherman in present-day Norway as follows:

The south-eastern lowlands and forest lands are inhabited by perch and pike, besides a number of coarse fish more or less widely distributed. A man content to angle for these fish would be able to get good sport in very beautiful surroundings in some of the south-eastern lakes.

The main eastern valleys from Telemark to Dovrefjeld will all offer opportunities for good trout if you go to the right places and to the remoter localities. But it is necessary to explore. From Telemark to the Gudbrandsdal trout is almost the only fish. Char has been largely introduced in the Gudbrandsdal. In these southern localities it does not take the fly very readily. The grayling is indigenous to the Gudbrandslaagen, the Glommen, and the Klara, and gives excellent sport, especially in the Fæmunden lake and the upper parts of the Klara.

Along the southern coast the lakes contain a mixed stock of perch and trout, besides occasionally char. The upper valleys and the mountains between them sometimes have good trout. The lakes of the Setesdal teem with the remarkable little dwarf salmon, a beautiful fish running up to half a pound.

All along the coast of Western Norway the inland waters are teeming with trout which, though small as a rule, give good sport to the man who likes to feel the fish tugging frequently at his line. Sport equal to that obtainable in the large Welsh reservoirs where so many British anglers seek pleasure is easily had in almost every lake or tarn along the west coast of Norway. In Western Norway, and going north along the coast, we find the char occurring more and more frequently and as a freer taker and a better sporting fish than in the south-east, until finally, somewhat south of the Polar Circle, we find it in the sea as well as in fresh water. Indeed, in Finmarken it is almost dominant in many localities. In this latter region where southern fish, pike and perch, also occur in places, we again meet the grayling, and in numbers which almost pass belief. A rise of grayling in one of the Finmarken rivers may be something almost incredible.

There is another noteworthy feature also about this extreme north of Norway. When leaving Trondhjem and the Namdal districts and going north, one enters into a region which becomes more and more primitive, more and more full of possibilities to the man of the magic wand. Much of it is still a vast wilderness frequented only by a few human beings, dependent on reindeer and grim nature's gifts of game and fish. Whoever ventures into this region will see primitive life and must live a primitive life.

Such, broadly speaking, is the fisherman's chances in the Norway of the present day. Hardly anywhere will he find the virgin grounds that charmed the old pioneers. In few places will he, as a matter of course, be able to make *very large* bags. Very seldom will he, unless he is a wealthy man and can afford to hire his own lake or hire a preserved fishing, be sure of getting very good sport. Almost everywhere the success of the fishing itself will be dependent on having experience and local knowledge. The success of the trip, however, is another matter. That is a mental affair depending on your own valuation of the whole business of your fly-fishing. Why do you fish? Surely not for the large bag. You fish for the joy of living in free nature, to enjoy the charm of the lake and stream, the blue or clouded sky, the mountains and the wind in the forest trees; and the expectancy, the anticipation of the bag, possibly the large bag. And Norway still can and will give it to the man who adventures. You must explore, you must pioneer—in a far wider sense and in a far more difficult way than fell to the lot of the old pioneers of the fly-rod in Norway.

[63]

CHAPTER VII

by

W. L. Calderwood

SALMON AND
SEA TROUT

"ANY fool can catch a salmon, but it takes a man to catch a trout" is a dictum I have had thrown at me. Yet when a man says he has caught a fish, we know, if we are in Scotland, that he means a salmon. In Newfoundland "a fish" means a cod, in the Arctic a whale. Here is an example of the usage in Newfoundland which I heard from a St. John's doctor.

A woman from the "outports"—one does not use the word "country" in an island where the people live on the coast and make a living by fishing—who had been in the doctor's care for some time began to sink, and, as her case was hopeless, the doctor telegraphed to her husband to come at once. In response he received a telegram which read: "Sorry cannot come. Am busy with the fish. Tell her I will meet her in heaven." Dr. Kegan was impressed by the certainty as to the place of meeting; but the message was sent in all simplicity and in perfect faith. What struck me was the expression "Am busy with the fish." The process of spreading out and turning over and stacking codfish is incessant along the shores of Newfoundland all the summer. Racks called "flakes" are used so that the fish may be raised above the ground, and on steep shores the flakes are terraced one above the other. The good soul had no longer his wife's help, so he was busy with the fish.

When a fishmonger erects a sign above his door, he does not go to a skilled artificer and say, "Make me a golden codfish." He asks for a salmon, not a silvery salmon, but a golden salmon; and the artificer generally makes him a precious bad one. Precious, because it is golden, but bad because the artificer likes curly fins and is obsessed by the mermaid idea. Sometimes we see a realistic representation of a salmon in golden wood or whatever the material is. Certain artists of the modern type would condemn the fish on this account, no doubt; but the fishmonger asked for a golden salmon, so the thing should be recognisable as a salmon. It is the trade sign with the king's image upon it, for the salmon is the king of fishes.

There are game fishes which are said to surpass the salmon. I am not referring at the moment to the cousin mentioned in the heading. (On light tackle *he* can give sport of a quality which I for one find difficulty in assessing; the salmon is the larger fish, but I doubt very much if it usually gives more sport.) I am thinking at the moment of dorado in fresh waters, and of those wonderful creatures of which I have merely read and heard, marlin and tuna, tarpon and swordfish, or of those immense skates which give such battle. I am thinking of all the wonderful marine sporting fishes of which Mr. Zane Grey writes.

But it seems to me that the difference in the value of the sport is very largely one of the temperament of the sportsman. You may prefer to hook a Leviathan which will fight for hours in the open sea and tow your launch nearly out of sight of land, or you may prefer to wade in a swirling river of ale-coloured water casting a fly for a trout or salmon, or to stand in a boat beyond trees and rocks plying your rod, as you listen to the lovely voice of running water, and see the shadows creep over the hills.

Also our equipment is the index to no small extent of the amount of sport we get out of our fishing. Do we fish for "tiddlers" or 30-pounders, our tackle must be ordered accordingly. There is a difference between catching to kill and catching for sport. Anyone can catch a shark if he baits suitably and has something like an anchor chain attached to the hook. It may be good fun, but it is not sport. In sporting fishing, the fish must have a sporting chance for its life. The late Mr. Tom Buckley made his famous score in the Helmsdale in the most sporting way. He used, if I recollect aright, a 14-foot trout rod and light tackle, or fairly light tackle, such as one would use when one expects the relatively small salmon of the Helmsdale. He could have doubled his score of twenty-two fish if he had used a strong rod and heavy tackle, for the fish were madly on the take. It was a day of a lifetime, though the sort of day that does not appear in the lives of most of us. He recognised this full well, but he was no fish-hog. When he broke his rod landing his fifteenth fish (he was alone) he went home, had some breakfast, and returned with a 12-foot rod. That was the decision of a true sportsman. How many of us would have hastened to get out a salmon rod and our strongest gut!

The 12- and 14-foot rod is now the length of the fashionable salmon wand. In the making of salmon rods in recent years they have become lighter in weight and shorter, without sacrificing strength. It suits boat or canoe work, but the short rod cannot lift a long line from the water as a longer rod with the weight well up can.

One cannot fish from the bank in most Canadian rivers, and a long rod is a disadvantage when a salmon has to be gaffed into a canoe. In the Grand Cascapedia and the Bonaventure, there is no place to land on if one looks for it. The rivers are cut through rock, and the trees hang closely over the upright rocky banks. The canoe is worked to the side of the river; the man at the upstream end hangs on to a branch or steadies the canoe with his pole, and the fish has to be brought to the man at the other end, who does the gaffing or netting.

On this subject of what really constitutes the sport we seek I am inclined to add, although I fear it is somewhat of a digression, that while the killing of the creature makes the natural climax, the absence of the killing does not deprive us of our sport. It is because I hold this view that I regard the fly as a more sporting lure than any spinning tackle which has in its make-up a bunch of hooks fixed in "triangle" fashion. If a salmon takes a minnow and the fish manages to break the trace, the unfortunate creature has still a horrible mouthful to get rid of.

We should elect of our own will to give the hunted creature a fair chance for its life. If a salmon beats us, we don't stop up the pool and drain off all the water so that we may certainly kill him. This is what the fox-hunter does when he digs out a fox gone to ground. The fox has given a good run, and the field should be content with it. If foxes become too numerous, shoot some of them, hunting country or no hunting country. It is a brutal business murdering a fox that has given a good run. It is on a par with killing the bull that has put up a great fight in the bull ring.

The man who is interested in his salmon at the end of his line does not pay much attention as a rule to the life of the fish in the sea. He likes to know that a rise in a river will bring up the fish, that it is not any use as a rule to fish in a rising river, that a water temperature round about 45° F. is a good one for fishing, and that in summer water fish run much faster than in the cold water of early spring. He likes to know the conditions under which fish surmount weirs and waterfalls, and the habits of fish in deep water and shallow, and where they take up their lies. He likes to know about the differences between spring fish and summer fish, and the ages of the fish he catches, and how often or seldom they have spawned. But the salmon in the sea is usually outside the angler's sphere of observation.

Every single salmon angler I have met, and hundreds I have not met, wish to talk about the non-feeding of salmon in fresh water. They think it is incredible that fish can starve for so long. It is a mercy our salmon look at our lures at all. The sockeye salmon in Pacific Coast rivers do not even do that.

They spawn once and die, and when they come from the sea they are apparently so intent upon the reproductive instinct that they have no inclination to look at anything which may even faintly resemble food, or which may attract them in any way from their one absorbing business.

But our Atlantic salmon does some wonderfully good feeding when he is in the sea. Herring, sprats, sand lances, and other fishes–on the Canadian shores, caplin and herring and sand lances–nourish him and make him grow. He also visits the bottom where crustaceans like shrimps and prawns are to be picked up. He does himself very well as a rule. He has good capacity, as many other fishes have. I have seen eight herring in the stomach of one salmon. He follows the herring shoals when he wants to feed on the herring, and he may go far off the land in doing so. What else does a salmon range the sea for?

He is to be found from the northern boundary of Portugal up to Iceland and Greenland, down to Labrador, Newfoundland, and Eastern Canada. He used to range to the Hudson River and beyond in former times, but only a remnant can now be traced in the rivers of the State of Maine. In that State, however, the landlocked variety has persisted in lakes, after the rivers had become too foul to allow of his migrating to and from the sea. By this I do not mean that he necessarily remained because the rivers had become foul. In Canada and Newfoundland the Ouaninich is found plentifully in lakes where there is no difficulty in the way of migrating to the sea. In Norway the Blege is literally cut off, and I have found the Ouaninich in the Terra Nova Lake in Newfoundland, which no migrating salmon can now reach owing to a 40-foot fall 3 miles below the outlet. The curious thing in the case of those Terra Nova fish was that they were kelts in the middle of August. They were without exception the leanest kelts I have seen, and on opening them I found that they had quite recently spawned, for a few undischarged ova were still in the abdominal cavity.

The migrating fish of these parts spawn in October and November, the fish of the Labrador in September and possibly later if the ice has not formed to prevent this. The ice is the great dominating factor. It delays the seaward migration of the smolts by reducing the food. Smolts are commonly three years old, are frequently four and sometimes five years. I found a $3\frac{1}{4}$-pound salmon, which had been a five-year-old smolt, had already spawned once after a year's sojourn in the sea, and had returned for another year after spawning. It was eight years old and $3\frac{1}{4}$ pounds.

The rainbow spawns in spring, as the steelhead also does, and most freshwater fishes do the same. The Ouaninich spawns in summer and is in good condition in spring, in Newfoundland. One specimen I examined at St. Andrews in the south of New Brunswick on June 10 showed no signs of summer spawning. The northern rivers often freeze to the bottom, and if the

Ouaninich frequents the smaller streams for spawning he will be unable to get into them in the normal spawning season, for ice forms in these streams early. In the interior of Newfoundland, the lonely uninhabited region from which the rivers flow, the winter temperature often falls to "20 below." The ice is probably the chief influence which has determined the change in the time of spawning, but there is another. The summer is relatively short. We have already seen that in many of the rivers where small salmon abound, the parr are poorly fed and the smolt stage is reached at a relatively late time, as it is in the Finmarken Province in the north of Norway. The recuperation of the Ouaninich after spawning would be a very slow process if the fish had to rely upon the early spring food. By spawning in summer it has the advantage of the greater amount of natural food to be found in the warmer months.

It is amazing to see the rapid growth of the plants when the warm weather comes at the end of May. Then the flies come out–and one can say a great deal about flies in Newfoundland, if one wants. I am told that the Labrador flies are as the sand of the sea for number, and that one does not really know about flies till one goes to the Labrador. One Canadian told me that he had seen the black flies so thick on a man's hands that it seemed as if he were wearing fur gloves. When the mosquitoes get numerous one is glad to see the dragon-flies getting busy, but the creatures that defy all screens in the evening are the "bite 'im and no see 'im" sand flies. Anyway, it is reasonable to suppose that amidst the multitude of flies the Ouaninich make a good living, and they would not get the flies if they spawned at the normal time.

The trout imported to New Zealand have had to change their time of spawning to suit the antipodal cold season. In the case of the Newfoundland Ouaninich the pendulum swings the other way. The winter pushes it back.

But the return of the migrating salmon from the sea is a romance. He seeks again his own river. Away out there far from land in the trackless ocean, he separates himself from his fellows who are still remaining with the flesh pots, and hies him back to the coast. Hundreds of miles he may have to swim, and he may not strike the coast anywhere near his own river, yet he has to find it. "Come I may, but go I must" was his spirit when he left the river, and now he comes again. It is a wonderful thing, this call of the river. We have no log of the salmon's wanderings in the sea, yet we know that, without a compass, he finds his way, and enters the old river ready to battle with rapids and waterfalls, aye, and ready to battle with those who throw attractive objects over him in which sharp steel is concealed.

We say it is his homing instinct that enables him to do this, but we simply, by this expression, supply a label for a thing we do not understand. Man has lost this instinct, this inner prompting which operates like conscience. We have gained intelligence, but lost instinct. In civilised life it is inevitable. The African natives whom Sir Frederick Lugard selected to aid him on his journeys could always point in the direction of the last camp, no matter how tortuous and hidden the track might have been. He learned that he could rely upon this absolutely for his direction. All he kept check of was his distance. I imagine no civilised man could do this. A donkey was once taken in a small sailing vessel from Gibraltar up the east coast of Spain. The vessel was wrecked, and a week afterwards the donkey walked into Gib. An Airedale dog, a great companion of mine, was taken in a closed car many miles out of Edinburgh to be left with friends while my house was closed during absence abroad. At two o'clock next morning he turned up, and was let in full of joy. It seemed hard to take him out again, but this time he understood. This is not a case of travelling by sight as a carrier pigeon is said to do. It is homing instinct like that of the salmon. The late Dr. Starr Jordan, the eminent American ichthyologist, would not allow the existence of this instinct in the salmon. He thought the fish did not go far from their rivers and would enter any convenient stream. He had not the benefit of the marking data we now possess. And as we extend our knowledge through marking fish in the sea we realise more and more the wide range of the salmon, and our imaginations are more stimulated thereby. We understand how *Salmo salar* is found on both sides of the Atlantic, and how *Oncorhynchus* is found on both sides of the Northern Pacific and the Bering Sea.

But char, which with us are now degenerate little salmonids, are the descendants of erstwhile large migratory fish. They are still migratory and large in the Arctic. The so-called brook trout of the American continent is a char, and like our trout in Europe descends to the sea and becomes the sea trout. By this I do not mean that it always does so, but that the sea trout of Eastern Canada and Newfoundland is the same fish as the creature which lives in fresh water (*S. fontinalis*).

The little colonies of char which now inhabit lakes in Britain were left there when the ice of the Glacial Period receded. They are like the little colonies of brown trout in certain streams of North Africa, which have managed to adapt themselves to gradually changing thermal conditions, though they have suffered in physique in the process.

Our sea trout have come to be fairly well understood in recent years. They occupy a position, as Mr. Nall has pointed out, midway between the salmon and the fresh-water trout, and they are of the same actual species as the latter. They love estuaries, where natural estuaries are to be found. They like to go in and out of brackish or fresh waters. They feed in fresh waters as salmon do not do, and they will drop back to the sea after visiting the upper waters of our rivers, or they will come in early in the season and stay in. They have a complicated variety of movements in different places. They may be said to have a tidal complex which operates from both directions, river and sea.

They sometimes grow rapidly and they sometimes grow slowly. At times they go farther away from their native coasts than we previously suspected. If the salmon's life is difficult enough to follow, the ongoings of the sea trout are much more so.

If one may take a leaf out of the book of a celebrated K.C., I would say:

> They sometimes look young although they are old;
> They sometimes are shy, and sometimes are bold;
>
> They sometimes go far and sometimes keep near;
> It's really not easy to make their ways clear.

Sea trout are the most enterprising fish I know. They will wait while the tide rises and will then struggle over a sandy beach into a little gutter of a stream the water of which is totally lost in the sand when the tide is out. They will climb up cascades where a salmon cannot possibly go because he draws so much water. And I have seen a sea trout that weighed only about 2 pounds take a vertical leap of 8 feet in order to clear a fall of 6.

In a little country like Britain, it is surprising that the trout often grow so large. I remember seeing the 29½-pound trout that was taken on a set line in Stenness in Orkney, when it was being set up by P. D. Malloch in Perth. That fish, no doubt like the others which frequent the tidal waters of the loch, had put on its weight in the sea. Yet it is even more amazing that so many very heavy trout have been taken in inland lochs from which it is unlikely that they went to the sea–fish, moreover, which had no appearance of having been to the sea. In the great lakes of the American continent, where one expects large things, fishes like these have never occurred.

We have all been familiar for years with the slob trout of Ireland, and in the days when Dr. Gunther reigned at the South Kensington Museum it was given specific distinction as *S. estuarius* (now departed from), yet I am not aware that even estuary feeding has produced fish as heavy as the Lough Erne trout of 32 pounds.

When I was netting the estuary of the Tay in pursuit of the smolt, and was drawing a sweep net on to the banks in the centre of the channel, I caught many trout up to about 3 pounds. They were in all possible stages between the ordinary brown trout and the sea trout, and some of the largest were quite yellow on the belly as if they had recently come down from fresh water, but they were all full of the young herring that were then in the Tay estuary. And now we find that the young sea trout in the whitling stage behaves in the same way, but again from the opposite direction, like the Ouaninich and the New Zealand trout. The whitling roams in from the sea and lives in tidal

M

lagoons for a time, then slips out again. This happens on the east coast of Scotland where there are tidal lagoons on several of the rivers. There are no such places at the mouths of west coast rivers, and spring trout go right in and stop there. Different kinds of places exhibit different habits in the trout which frequent them. We are dealing with a very plastic species. In their west coast habit, the sea trout behave just as the salmon do.

The young stage of the salmon, on its first return from the sea, still presents features of difficulty. We see the grilse in our country returning to their rivers in June and July and August and September, and if we fish, as I have done in the most shameless way with a net, during the annual close time, we find them still coming in during October and November. These late fish are just ready to spawn, and they breed late progeny.

In some rivers grilse do not appear at all. This is still a mystery. In other rivers during the open season the great majority of the grilse are males. In the Rhine the St. Jacob's Zalm are believed to be all males. In the Ristigouche the superintendent tells me he has never seen a grilse with spawn. I asked him to try at spawning time. In Scotland there is no trouble about getting female grilse at any time when grilse are to be had. When ripe they produce about 500 eggs per pound weight of the fish, and in rivers like the Tay one may see odd grilse that run up to about 10 pounds, and are heavier than very many of the older spring salmon of the small class.

In the rivers of Eastern Canada and Newfoundland grilse are usually very small–2, 3, and 4 pounds. In the Grand Cascapedia there are none. It is a big fish river with an average weight for rod-caught fish of 23 pounds. In the Hampshire Avon there are none, it is said; I have no experience of the river. In the rivers of the Pacific Coast grilse appear to be precocious juveniles that accompany the normal runs of salmon. There are no runs of grilse as we know them, but a certain number of those precocious fish accompany their elders when they leave the sea. The grilse of coho and of dog or chum salmon are only in their second year, and they are all males. Now it has sometimes been noticed in Britain that precocious male smolts occur, and that they can fertilise the eggs of female salmon. Ripe female smolts, in natural conditions, have never been found. They have been induced, however, under the influence of high living in ponds.

The explanation of all this seems to be that a reserve of the male element is necessary in many places to maintain the species. Mortality at spawning time is far greater amongst males than amongst females. I am not speaking about creatures like the sockeye which all die after spawning. A few grilse sockeye also occur, but although the great majority are males, it appears that females do occur amongst them. It may make little difference in the case of the sockeye if there is an excess of females unpaired. In British rivers we find every now and again creatures that are called "egg-bound," because at a late date their eggs are still unshed. In some districts they are called Rawners. I have seen them as late as the end of May. These are simply late-running females which have failed to find mates. I remarked many years ago that the male kelts were the first to leave the river, that by the month of March almost all the kelts one meets are females. The males that by then are not safely back in the sea are dead. Smolts do not leave fresh waters till the end of May, as a rule, so the precocious males amongst them would be of service to late females. The late-running grilse appear to me to be in the same category. The males are often ripe before the females, as in the case of the smolts, and on this account they run into fresh waters. They can penetrate to small head streams where large salmon seldom go, and they can there pair off with females that otherwise would be unattended. *Contra nando incrementum,* as the legend of a certain ancient and royal burgh has it below the coat of arms with three salmon, one swimming up and two swimming down again. The local fishermen, who know only too well the habits of certain lieges who seek out the salmon on their spawning beds with "clips" and "leisters," say the motto really means that for two salmon that swim up only one comes back again.

It is an amazing thing, this pursuit of the spawning salmon. Right through its life the fish is pursued. Even when the fish is creating more of its kind for the use of man, men go and kill it. One can understand a situation in which Indians are allowed to spear salmon at all times, because they have dogs that are necessary to them in winter and which have to be fed on the salmon. But this bloodthirsty desire to kill, be it a rare bird, a large animal, or a salmon which having braved all dangers has at last reached the spawning beds, is beyond reason, without intelligence. It is the primitive impulse reappearing, the savage dregs of the hunting instinct when man had to kill to live, and when man showed his superiority amongst the animals by his power of killing.

In the experience of all of us, as in the experience even of an ex-inspector of salmon fisheries who, in the words of a candid friend, has "done his damnedest" to prevent such things, it is known that some people seem to be unable to resist the temptation to kill fish when they find fish in their power, and to kill them in any old way. I have known men who cursed the fish they could not catch, and who, when no one was looking, deliberately stroke-hauled them with a weighted hook, and who afterwards had the nerve to say what fly they killed each fish on, etc. And, forsooth, angling is called the gentle art. . . .

The caribou of Newfoundland have had to be protected, recently, by a close time which will last at any rate for five years and probably for much longer, because certain "sports" went out by the railway to the place where the caribou annually crossed in the fall, and slaughtered them, leaving the carcases

[75]

to rot on the ground. These "sports" are no sportsmen, but they are akin to the folks who would kill salmon at spawning time.

I would beg, therefore, that when we go out in pursuit of the salmon and its game cousin the trout, we do so for sport and not primarily to kill.

An American who has killed sporting fish in sea and river in many parts of the world, and who has now largely given it up, tells me that he would like to buy a salmon river and leave the fish alone. Anglers are apt to be philosophers after all.

CHAPTER VIII

by

F. Gray Griswold

SALMON FISHING IN CANADA

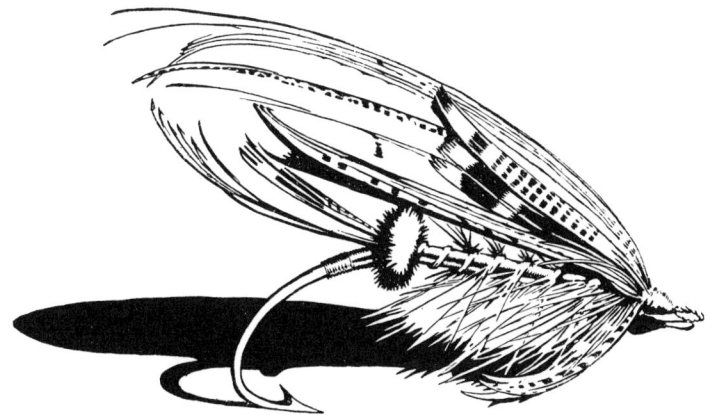

THE conditions of salmon fishing in Canada differ greatly from those in Great Britain. I believe the reason why this sport has had such a vogue in Great Britain and why so many books on the subject have been written is that the salmon has been known there and respected since the days before the Romans, and that owing to wise laws and their observance it is still to be found plentifully in many British rivers.

It is the proximity of these rivers to the abodes of the anglers that has made the sport so popular. In some cases the stream is at the foot of the angler's lawn, so that when his gillie informs him that the water has cleared and fallen after a spate, he has but to pull on his waders, stroll down to the pool, and fish. We have to journey two days by rail to reach the nearest salmon water.

Then the fishing, owing to the comparative absence of hard frost, and to a more or less continuous run of fish at all seasons, is possible from February until November.

When my ancestors in the seventeenth century arrived at the mouth of the Connecticut River, with the Say and Brook expedition, to settle on the land granted to the noble lords of those names, they found the river alive with both salmon and shad. There are records of a later date that relate the fact that when a man wished to buy a shad from the fishermen, he was obliged to purchase two salmon at a small price in order to obtain the highly prized shad. These were the conditions in those days in almost every river from what is now the State of Maine to the Delaware River in the south.

It was not many years before these conditions changed, for by constructing dams in order to run their grist- and saw-mills the settlers prevented the salmon from reaching their spawning beds, and the few remaining fish were destroyed

[79]

by sawdust and other pollution of the rivers. Today a very few salmon are still to be found in the two most easterly rivers in Maine only.

It was a sad destruction of great future wealth, not to mention the possibilities of sport with rod and fly.

As the salmon had all been destroyed, angling with us was developed chiefly by fishing for the *fontinalis*, which is commonly called a trout, but which is really a member of the *char* family.

The development of our fishing tackle, which is now celebrated, was greatly influenced by the very game sea fish called in these waters the striped bass, and known further south as the rockfish (*Roccus lineatus*). It was this fishing that developed the multiplying reel and taught us properly to estimate the strain that can be safely put on rod and line.

The first records we have of salmon fishing in Canada date from the fifties of the last century, but it no doubt existed earlier in those rivers which flow into the St. Lawrence just east of Quebec, but which now hold no salmon.

The first authentic records are of the Godabout and the Moisie, two north shore St. Lawrence rivers. Anglers from the United States began in the fifties to take the long journey north for the purpose of enjoying fly-fishing for salmon, and they left records of some of their yearly catches.

In the seventies and eighties the demand for salmon fishing increased rapidly. Rich Americans bought and leased rivers in the provinces for that purpose, and as it became more and more expensive to fish those streams, they founded fishing clubs and built camps along the rivers to accommodate their angling members.

It is this procedure which has preserved the salmon fishing as it exists in the province of Quebec today, for where the public has been allowed free fishing, or where they were simply taxed by a small yearly license fee, as in Nova Scotia and parts of New Brunswick, the rivers have been practically depleted of salmon. In Quebec the lessees of the rivers have bought most of the nets in the tidal waters, but in Nova Scotia and New Brunswick netting in the fresh water is allowed. The St. John River is netted for over 120 miles from its tidal waters. How any fish manage to work their way past these many nets is a problem, but they do, and a few are found as high up as Grand Falls, 225 miles from the sea.

Added to these depredations, the salmon are now not even allowed to reach their rivers, for they are drift-netted off shore in the sea as well.

In 1929 there were 84,950 fathoms of drift-nets in the Gulf of St. Lawrence. The politicians claim they cannot refuse anyone *who has a vote* a license to fish. The consequence is, the Miramichi, once a great salmon river, now holds few fish, and at no far distant time most of the other salmon rivers in Canada will be in a like condition. The golden egg hangs by a silken cord.

Our fishing season is a short one. Its beginning depends on the arrival of the salmon after the ice goes out. The fish seem to run up stream when the temperature of the river water suits them. This usually happens about the second week in June. The season closes on August 15, excepting in a few rivers in New Brunswick. The Indians are allowed to fish in the St. John River until October 1, but the salmon they take during the last few weeks are black fish.

As the rivers in Canada are for the most part too deep and too swift to wade, one must fish them from canoes, for the trees grow down to the water's edge and bank fishing is impossible.

The angler has a great advantage over a hooked salmon when fishing in a canoe, for the canoe is dropped down at once below the hooked fish.

The killick is lowered at the head of a pool, or wherever the first spot is that is known at times to hold salmon. This depends on the height of the water, as salmon change their positions according to the strength of the stream. The guides are well acquainted with such matters and place the canoe according to custom. As you cast your fly over the waters the canoe is gradually lowered down stream by giving it rope, and by lifting the killick, allowing the canoe to float down stream, and anchoring again. Each pool has a given number of drops according to the height of the water.

When a salmon is hooked the killick is lifted and the canoe is paddled to the river bank where the angler plays his fish and where his guide gaffs it. In case a fish takes down stream the canoe follows.

The book tells one that it should take one minute to the pound to kill a salmon. This is in my opinion an overestimate, and I believe the limit should be just half that time under Canadian conditions of fishing.

I was already an experienced sea fisherman when I began to fish for salmon, and was used to handling the most modern tackle invented for the taking of heavy game fish. I was greatly surprised to find that fly-fishing tackle had only slightly changed in the last hundred years, and that the anglers followed the English authorities implicitly. As our conditions are quite different, I changed my methods of fishing in order to make the task easier, and to obtain more personal action and pleasure.

My fishing companion and I travelled up and down the Grand Cascapedia River for nine seasons and fished the same waters diligently for a month each year.

We met at an early breakfast, and again at a late dinner, after which we usually sat by the fire and often discussed the well-worn subject of salmon fishing. It was the only subject on which we did not agree, so we were therefore the more inclined to discuss it.

The proof that we were both right in our ideas on the subject is that, by a

N

very strange coincidence, at the end of the ninth season we found we had each taken the same number of fish, namely 559 salmon in nine years.

We differed in opinion because my companion was a Fundamentalist and I was a Modernist. He had read almost every book that had been written on the subject by Englishmen, from Izaak Walton to Arthur Hutton, faithfully followed their advice, and fished according to Hoyle.

I, on the contrary, although I had also read those books, believed that the advice given by these great authorities was correct for their own conditions, but as the conditions in Canada were different other methods should there be employed.

My companion was an old salmon fisherman with much skill and experience. I was an experienced sea fisherman who had taken up fly-fishing late in life, and who had taught himself to cast. I had no prejudices.

He fished with a rather limber rod, 14 feet long; I usually used a stiff 13-foot rod, known as a wind rod, intended to fish with in a strong upstream wind. He used a single action reel and changed the drag from time to time. My reel was a multiplyer. I fished without a drag and controlled my fish with my left thumb on the cork handle of the rod above the reel. With a thumb-stall I could feel the fish and graduate the pressure, which you cannot do with a drag without often changing it. His bending, bobbing rod had most of the fun which should have been his; whereas I enjoyed all this pleasure in my hands and arms.

My companion carried a box with numerous patterns and sizes of flies; I used but three or four patterns and sizes. In fact, to prove my contention that it did not matter what fly one used as long as one gave it a chance, I had a private fly made which I called the "Griswold Gray." On three sizes of this fly I took 415 of the total of 559 salmon. I believe there is more in the presentation of a fly than in its many-coloured feathers.

My friend fished sitting down in his canoe; I always stood up when casting. He hooked his fish from the reel-brake; I held my line on the rod with the second finger of the right hand, and did not strike until I felt sure the salmon was hooked, but then I struck hard. In that way one loses all lightly hooked fish at once instead of later on.

He changed hands in casting right or left. I never changed hands when casting.

If he simply rose a salmon without pricking it he would give it a good long rest, change the fly in size, and often in pattern, and continue this if the fish came again.

I seldom changed my fly in any circumstances and seldom rested a fish. If I rose a fish short I gave it the fly again at once. If the fish did not take it then I stripped line and fished the drop out and then came back to the first rise.

This gives a salmon a long rest, but you miss this opportunity if you hook a fish below on the same drop.

I asked my companion one day why he lowered his rod when a fish jumped. He said that it was the correct thing to do in order to give the salmon line, because the fish is trying to break the cast by hitting the line with its tail. In this case I lift the line and give no slack. My friend's method of lowering his rod whenever a salmon jumped is the custom when a man is above his fish, in the water or on the bank of a stream, as the strain is then a direct one to the jumping salmon. In those circumstances it is well to lower the tip. Our conditions are, however, quite different. When we hook a fish the canoe is dropped down stream and paddled ashore. Our fish when they jump are usually across stream or above us. If you attempt to give line the current takes it, and the salmon is back in the stream before the slack reaches it. If you have a strong drag on your reel at that moment there is an excessive strain on your tackle when the fish makes its next move. I fancy the proper theory is to drop your tip if a salmon jumps with its head away from you, but not to do so if the head is pointing towards you. This needs a quicker eye than I have.

My friend adapted the size of the flies he used to the conditions of light and water and gave it great thought.

I am a believer in large flies and seldom used a fly smaller than a 3/o. I would begin the season with a 6/o, change later to a 4/o and 3/o double. In low-water conditions I went to the other extreme and used 6's and 8's double.

When the salmon were rising short and just nipping I found a double hook would cure them of this bad habit.

One season I took forty-eight large salmon on one "Griswold Gray" 4/o and cast without untying fly or cast. Another year I landed thirty salmon (weighing 746 pounds) on a 3/o double of the same pattern, two fish being over 40 pounds each.

In the early season I usually fished with a twisted gut collar 1½ yards long, and a stout gut leader of the same length. This was done because this taper casts well and in order to "horse" the many heavy hooked kelt. At the end of my line I wrap a loop, and between that and the gut cast I place a small brass ring. This is most handy and avoids all tying and untying of knots or cutting of line. The ring weighs less than a knot and creates no bubbles when working the fly, but its greatest advantage is that it blocks when it reaches the end of the tip and does away with all watching of line knot. It is a great comfort to the angler.

This simply proves that there is more than one method of taking salmon with a wet fly in strong water. Other conditions, other methods.

I had a guide who could cast and fish a fly much better than I could, but

[83]

who would seldom hook a salmon, for he struck too soon and pulled the fly away from the disappointed fish.

I was amused this summer watching three Indians fishing in New Brunswick with heavy self-made rods. They cast beautifully and fished well until they hooked a salmon. Then they seemed to lose their presence of mind, for they pointed their rods at the salmon and killed or lost the fish on the reel. However, they landed twenty-one salmon in one day, in one pool.

As it takes a novice some time to distinguish the difference between a Silver Grey and a Mar Lodge, I hardly think a fresh run salmon can do so. I believe one should use a smaller fly in shallow pools than in deep waters. When fishing with a long line it is well to pull in some line before lifting it for the next cast, for it saves the rod, which is important for the light rods we now use. If you wish to fish a deep fly it is well to shoot some line as the fly falls, and to cast well down stream. One seldom knows how deep one's fly fishes, but it is a known fact that is seldom recognised that a light line sinks better than a heavy one. The finer the line the less surface it has and therefore the less resistance to the stream.

I believe in killing a salmon as quickly as possible, by playing it hard, for the longer a fish is on, the greater is the chance of losing it. My advice is, keep your rod-tip up, and as much of your line as possible out of water and near the surface. More salmon are lost by gentle treatment than by playing them too hard. In the last ten years' fishing I have not broken a single tip, nor can I remember parting a leader. I have lost flies that had been tied in a hurry by cold fingers and I split two butts fighting big kelt. But there is always a slip of the line in my method and no sudden jerk, as there is at times from a reel-brake.

The worst emergency with which an angler has to deal in playing a fish is that of a "jigging salmon." One has an active reply to the salmon's every other move, but in the case of jigging a passive endurance is the only possible response. The short, heavy jerks at intervals of but a few seconds are apt to have a most demoralising effect upon the angler's nerves.

How and why does the salmon do it? Is it opening and shutting its mouth, gasping for breath? Is it standing on its head trying to rub the fly free against a stone, or simply swinging its head angrily from side to side? I have never been able satisfactorily to decide these questions.

I meditated this matter as I sat by the fire one evening at Middle Camp on the Grand Cascapedia River trying to dry my sodden clothes after an evening's angling in the rain. I had been fishing Little Camp pool, and had risen and hooked a heavy fish which had sulked and jigged until eventually we parted company.

While I was deep in thought my fishing companion, who had been up stream, arrived in a somewhat drowned condition. I asked him the question which was in my mind. He laughed and said, "Let me tell you of an experience I once had with jigging."

He lit his pipe and sat down.

"I was bound down stream," he said, "one evening in my canoe, and as I passed through Dewinton's pool I chanced to see what I believed to be a 50-pound salmon (but of course they always look big when in the river). One could easily recognise that fish if seen again by a long white mark on its shoulder, which was evidently an old, healed gill-net wound.

"I said to my fisherman: 'George, we must follow that fish up stream and try to capture him. Tomorrow will be Sunday. By Monday morning that fish should be in Big Camp pool.'

"It was early in the season, and I was the only member of the Club on the river, so Monday morning we poled up stream and fished the better part of Big Camp, taking several good fish, but seeing no sign of our stout friend. The men had their supper at Middle Camp, and I had a welcome cup of tea. After the sun had gone down we had a try in the famous pool in front of this camp. On the second drop I hooked a fish below the surface that did not show. The killick was lifted, and we moved as usual to the shore a little below the fish. When I lightened my line I appreciated that I had a heavy fish, and at once I thought of the scarred giant. I believed the fish would soon come to terms, as it appeared to be hanging in the current, but it suddenly began to jig to beat the band, and then I was sure I had hold of a sulking fish on the bottom. Having often been told that when a salmon jigged it was a certain sign that the fish was lightly hooked, I did not put much strain on the tackle for a time, but I stepped ashore and tried to move His Majesty by pressure from below, and then from up stream, but all to no effect.

"As I am not blessed with an over-supply of patience, I then proceeded to give the salmon all the butt my tackle would stand. The more I did this the harder the salmon jigged. It was now nearly dark, and the negro cook came down from the house to tell me that it was nine o'clock and that my dinner was getting cold. I handed the rod to George, my guide, who had been standing near, gaff in hand, watching the struggle.

"I told him to have a try, but that I believed I was fast to a log. He said: 'No, no; it is a salmon all right, and a big one. I never felt a fish with so strong a jig.'

"After dinner I lighted a cigar and strolled down to the pool in the moonlight. I found George up a tree on the bank. He was lashing the handle of the rod, above and below the reel, to a limber branch. When he came down he said: 'The rod is safe, the reel is clear, and it has a good drag on it; by daylight that fish will be floating dead on the surface, or else he will have worked the fly out of his jaw.' We all turned in.

[85]

"In the morning, bright and early, we found the rod still in place, and the tip showed plainly that the fish was still jigging. George untied the rod and handed it down, and we took to the canoe again. I told the bowman to drop his killick above the fish and give us rope enough to allow George to try and poach the salmon with his gaff. At that moment the sun began to shine above the eastern hills. George looked down into the pool and said the water was too deep, that his gaff would not reach, and that we must go ashore for a moment. He ran up to the house and soon appeared with a rope and the ice-tongs. We moved back into the pool, anchored, and allowed the canoe to drift astern to the proper spot. George lowered the ice-tongs and with some difficulty pulled up a loose coil of barbed wire with my hook fast to one end of it. The guides both laughed heartily when I remarked: 'That settles it—the jig is up!'"

CHAPTER IX

by
John C. Moore

THE MAGNIFICENCE
OF THE CHUB

THE purists, the aristocrats of the fly-rod, will scorn him and abuse him, and if one of them should catch you on your way down to the river with that old greenheart which has a glorious kink in its top joint, he will set his nose high and condemn you also. The chub, he will say, is no quarry for a gentleman; but is a craven fish without honour, that comes like a sheep to the slaughter, that fights not at all when hooked, and is slimy withal, uneatable, and inordinately full of bones; a creature, in short, only fit for tyros to practise upon, and one which stinks in the nostrils of all honourable men. He will probably hint also that poor Loggerhead is cannibalistic, that he devours spawn, and finally (since we are all so insular as to try to make out our enemies to be foreigners) that he is an alien in British waters.

You will do well to treat the purist to some excessively vulgar gesture, such as making a long nose at him, which will leave him so flabbergasted that he can think of no adequate reprisal. He is ill-equipped, poor chap, to combat such measures, but they are the only proper answer to his jabber.

You may now go your own way unmolested down to the river and to your chub. Only you and a few select others know him for what he is—the gallant fellow who takes a fly as if he meant it, and then as he feels the hook goes off like a demon in a strong rush for the bank and the willow-roots; the companion of bright June days and of bat-haunted summer twilights, the inhabitant of delightful places, the whole rhyme and reason, in fact, of all the loved business of slipping down river into flaming dawns between ranks of misty willows, and of the gentle swish of the rod, and of the memorable plash of oars into the

o

molten stuff which sunshine makes of the ripples. . . . But these are mysteries not meet for explanation; we chub fishers are the esoteric company; and it is the purists who are the mob without, the Philistines.

Were I to catalogue all the awful things they have said about the chub, I verily believe that the print of this page would become scarlet and smoulder and vanish in smoke; and the calumnies are almost all untrue, because they are based upon misconceptions. For instance, the proper habitat of the chub is in great rivers like the Severn and the Thames; and I shall be the first to admit that in a dry-fly stream such as the Coln or Windrush his presence is a bit of a nuisance. His nice sense of humour leads him to secrete himself beneath an almost inaccessible tree and then to rise, all day long, in the manner of a large trout; and when you have changed your fly many times (often of necessity, owing to certain unfriendly boughs) he comes at it with a rush, leading you to expectation of high things, only to shatter your hopes when he shows himself in his true colours a moment later. All this is apt to warp your judgment. Therefore, when we speak of the chub, let us imagine him in a broad river where no trout are, lying in the swift weirs or beneath the tall willows that overhang the banks.

In such a river his importance is considerable. He exists there as a sort of living sign and symbol that fish may really be caught on the fly. Small boys who have never wholly believed this magnificent fact borrow their fathers' fly-rods, pass through agonies of despair, and are finally converted when old Loggerhead—out of his infinite charitableness—deigns at last to rise to the draggled soldier-palmer hurled heavily at his nose.

I spent my early youth in a barren and troutless country, and though all through the summer many a rod was to be seen in the streets of the little town where I lived, very few of them were fly-rods. From the bottom of the garden I could see the place—not 400 yards away—where the Warwickshire Avon joined the great Severn; and half a mile below that estuary there was the steady roar of Tewkesbury Weir. Leviathan himself, thought I, must lurk in those swirling waters; but for me Leviathan was clad in the guise of pike and perch and roach and chub, for there were no trout in that place, and the famous Severn salmon, being uncatchable on the rod, did not come into my reckonings.

Therefore, although by my eighth birthday I knew much about paste and fat worms and stewed wheat, and more than many small boys about the unholy mysteries connected with wasp-grubs and maggots (genteelly called gentles), I knew nothing at all about the little bunches of feathers which are the true symbols of the angler's craft. I had heard of fly-fishing vaguely, as a sort of mystic cult which was practised in distant places; it seemed to me to be something magical and unreal, akin to the passes of a wand in a fairy-story.

Then, a year later, I saw a man actually practising it in a boat below the weir; but he caught nothing, and though I was fascinated by the graceful movements of his slender rod and the lovely curve of his line, which shone like a spider's thread in the sunlight, I had no serious wish to emulate him. I decided that fly-fishing was but another of the silly and unprofitable games which my elders played, like tennis and golf.

When I was ten, however, a benevolent uncle, meeting me as I carried my bamboo roach rod down to the river, pulled an old mayfly out of his deerstalker hat and presented it to me. He assured me that it had actually caught fish; and though I hardly believed him, I tied it to my gut cast and spent all the morning flicking it fruitlessly into the river. Once a bold inquisitive minnow followed it, and gave me encouragement. Incredible as it seemed, evidently the strange contraption possessed some interest for the fishy kind; so then I took it to a railway bridge which spanned the Avon at a place where large chub frequently lay on hot days–sleepy monsters who seemed dead until you showed your face over the bridge, when they woke into frenzied life and scattered in a second.

My mayfly had already lost half its hackle and one of its wings, and was a sorry-looking object indeed. I crept to the edge of the bridge and peeped over. The chub were still there, dark greenish shapes with slightly tremulous fins. I hid myself, and lowered my fly until it touched the water; and then suddenly there was a splash and a tug and a fearful heaving. I hauled up a $\frac{3}{4}$-pounder hand over hand.

I sometimes think that fish are specially kind to small boys. Were I to try to do the same thing nowadays, I am sure my gut would break or the hook lose its hold. And probably there are no chub at all under the railway bridge now. . . . Why is it that fish never seem so large or so plentiful as they were in days gone by? Does memory wear rose-coloured spectacles? And was the Leviathan of our youth but a 3-pound pikelet? I do not know. There were perch in many a little pond in those days, and there are few perch now; and the chub were everywhere then, whereas they are hard to seek today. *Mais où est le neige d'antan?* I ask; and I think most fishermen would echo me. Where, indeed?

My $\frac{3}{4}$-pound chub, who had given his life blindly–like a sacrifice to Juggernaut–in order that I might become a true angler, was the only one I had that morning, but he was enough. I had in my bedraggled mayfly the unshakeable and fanatical faith of the recently converted; my uncle, the giver of it, took on in my mind the proportions of a god.

And so I became, by slow steps, a fly-fisherman. At first it was a matter of dangling a mayfly over bridges; and then of dapping a palmer between the branches of the willows; and then of hurling it out on to the shallows where the roach lay on hot days. It was not until I was sixteen that I possessed a proper greenheart fly-rod, and not until a year later that I was taught how to use it; but these were mere details. The date of my conversion was the date of that hot summer day when I was ten.

I never saw a trout till I was seventeen, but in my Severn and Avon I had a great variety of other fishes to practise upon. The chub came first and fore-most always, of course; but I soon discovered that the roach would snap up a small fly willingly in low water and hot weather, when they lay on the surface in dark-backed shoals. Later, I found by accident that the water-gods had provided little dace in plenty to teach me that the hand and eye of an angler must be as quick as a rackets-player's; and finally, I found that a gaudy fly dragged backwards and forwards among the weeds would trick a perch, or even a little pike, into thinking that it was a minnow.

Indeed, I sometimes wonder whether there is any fish, in any part of the world, that could not be caught on some kind of fly. Eels have been known to take a wet-fly, I know; carp too, and even, I believe, one or two phenomenal bream! As for minnows and bleak and rudd, they are easy prey. Gudgeon and daddy-ruffs I am doubtful about; but they are omnivorous beasts, and I daresay that sometime when the moon is blue the thing will be accomplished.

In mid-June last year I received from the artist whose delightful drawings decorate this book an urgent and imperative request for fishes, a great variety of fishes, to serve as his models and to give him "ideas." Postcards arrived daily demanding roach, dace, chub, and trout; perch and pike too, if they could come legitimately into the scope of a book on the fly-rod. (And of course they could–even if they couldn't, how could we leave out the two most decorative fish found in English waters?)

I was very busy at that time, and could not spare a whole day on which to experiment with a variety of rods and baits. I had but four hours of a summer evening, and therefore I took with me to the river a fly-rod, and a fly-rod only.

I knew the water well, almost every inch of it, so I went straight to all the likely spots. I had a small chub and dace pretty quickly; I caught a minnow on a little black gnat, and with him as bait (lip-hooked on a stripped mayfly) I got a greedy little perch out of a favourite waterfall. The black gnat later lured another dace which, sunk deep among the lily-stems, produced a 2-pound jack who gave my fine gut and my 10-foot greenheart rod a battle which will live long in my memory.

I was rather proud of that single evening's work! But pride soon had a fall, for the roach eluded me for a week, and when at last I caught him and put him in a box and sent him off, some hiatus in the posts delayed him, so that even the postman who delivered him to Mr. Sheringham suggested diffidently that "there might be summat wrong with this 'ere package."

There was; and the weather was hot. I am very glad that I was not present when daylight was let in upon that roach.

But Mr. Sheringham did a very courageous thing. He knew not when I might catch another roach, and such was his devotion to his art that he tied a handkerchief round his nose and mouth and painted the fish in the garden. Half an hour later it was buried. . . .

The result is one of the drawings which adorn this book.

The trout continued to elude me; and it must be confessed that finally, in desperation, I drove over to Mr. Severn's fish farm on the Cotswolds and begged a fine fish from there. Those were days of blazing sun, and the fly-rod had met its match.

Although, as we have seen, almost all kinds of coarse fish may be caught on the fly-rod, the chub still remains the chief quarry of them all. With the exception of rudd and dace, the capture of the others is usually an accident and a phenomenon; but the chub is really important, because for so many of us he is the teacher of our youth, the prophet who converts us to a new faith. He is a symbol of all fishes everywhere. It is he who sets our feet in the way which leads towards Tweed and Tay and Torridge, towards Welsh lake and Scottish loch and Irish river. It is from him that we begin to learn the part which the fly-rod can play as one of life's better things, until later we realise that its importance is such that it may even be an ambassador of friendship between two nations, as it has been between Britain and Norway.

Let us get back, therefore, to the chub of our youth, and the methods we must use to catch them.

In a big river a boat is indispensable, though there may be places where you can get a good fish now and then by dapping a fly in between the trees from the high bank, or where you can wade far out on sandy shallows; but if you want a chance of the big chaps, and are going to do the thing seriously, you will do well to invest in some sort of a craft, which to my mind should be just big enough to hold one occupant—namely, yourself. Two men in a boat can hardly ever be quiet enough for the job; but this is a matter of taste, I know, and also of experience, because unless you are a practised waterman you will upset the little cockleshell before very long, and if you are a dreamer you may shoot a weir in it. But it is a fairly easy matter, when you become used to the oars, to manage a small boat and to fish at the same time; although if you are one of those folk who catch crabs or stand on the seat in midstream or try to jump through the floor-boards I recommend you to a large ship's dinghy or to a barge if you can get hold of one.

There is a popular fallacy which supposes fly-fishing for chub to be an affair both elephantine and barbarous when compared with the high art of luring a trout with a floating dun or olive. It is imagined that all that is necessary is to heave a very large fly, made in the fashion of a bumble-bee but resembling no known creature, very violently in the direction of the chub's tail; whereupon (the fallacy goes) he will turn greedily and take it in a monstrous swirl. What actually happens is that he does just as you would do if you were swimming peacefully along and someone loosed a hundredweight sack of coal at your behind. In effect he says to himself, in the well-chosen words of Malcolm: "Let us not be dainty of leave-taking, but shift away." So great is his hurry that he makes a splash; and this vastly pleases the angler, who thinks he has risen at the fly. I have actually seen this happen time and again.

No: catching chub with a fly may be easy, but it's not as easy as all that. In clear water they are as shy as trout, and a bungled cast or a careless movement which throws a shadow will send them flashing away. White garments are fatal in fishing for them; and to cast with a bright sun behind you is equally an antidote to sport. They are not often gut-shy, but I have known them to be so now and then, and there is no reason at all to use gut thicker than 4x. On this you should not often lose a fish that is properly hooked, yet it is fine enough to make it necessary to play your chub carefully.

Although a wet fly will serve most purposes in most rivers, and is the only practicable method in very swift water below weirs and falls, I must confess that I never use it for chub except occasionally in rough water or high wird I do not assert that the dry fly will catch more fish, though on hot days and in still dawns and dusks it usually wins hands down; but the point is that one fishes for pleasure, and not as a business, and the dry fly is infinitely better fun. Your palmer or spent gnat floats down over a likely backwater between two willow bushes; you watch it anxiously, and then all of a sudden it just isn't there. You have not seen it disappear, but there is a broad dark nose poked up instead. Then the snout vanishes in its turn with a slight "plop," leaving a single big bubble and a few rings chasing each other outwards. You tighten, and then the reel starts singing. The rod becomes alive in your hands, and you are playing your chub; but the important point is that very rarely, save in the case of small fish, does the splash happen until *after* your fish is hooked or lost as the case may be. Nine people out of ten, on their first day's chub-fishing, strike too soon. Actually the chub takes a fly very slowly indeed. Dace snap at it, and roach I have found erratic, sometimes quick and sometimes leisurely, but chub always take their time. It is a thing well worth remembering.

The question of flies is an extremely interesting one. It has been asserted that chub are indiscriminating—that they will rise at anything within reason if they are in a mood to rise at all; also, that if by chance they have any preference, it is for a very large and woolly palmer, with a red or white tail. I have

found this only partially true; for while they certainly do not ever demand an exact imitation of the fly on the water, there are occasions in time of drought and hot weather when it pays to use small trout flies. During the hot summer of 1929 I discovered that often, in the middle of the day, nothing but a little black gnat would fetch them; but that in the early morning and late evening, particularly if there was a slight breeze, they came better to the coachman and coch-y-bonddhu and the standard palmers. Nevertheless, I am quite sure that most of the patterns sold as "chub flies" in local tackle-shops are too big. They are difficult to cast accurately, particularly in a wind; they hit the water with a fearful splash, and moreover they are inclined to fray the cast. There is a happy medium, I am certain, between the little black gnat and the monster bumble-bee; and I for one would be positively ashamed to offer any fish some of the enormous fuzzy abominations which one sees in the shops. Most of these are supposed to represent the great furry caterpillars–"drinkers," "withy-bobs" (larvæ of the buff-tip moth), and the delightfully named "woolly bears"–to which chub are so partial; but as all these caterpillars sink immediately when they fall off trees into the water, imitations of them used dry cannot be justified on entomological grounds!

The really big chub are not to be taken on the dry fly: 3-pounders will have it now and then (I had two such with successive casts below a weir in Shakespeare's Avon on an unforgettable morning last summer, and have been drinking beer to their memory ever since); 4-pounders vouchsafe themselves very rarely to the Chosen of God, but before you have caught one you will have seen many summer dawns and watched the sun sink down evening after evening behind the far hills, and endured much travail in the attainment of the magic known as Quietude. For big chub are a strange and secret race; they are a company of dark shadows, like immortal spirits. You come upon them suddenly, in groups of four and five, and you are so staggered, so taken aback at the sight of them, that you think it has all been a dream when the last of them sinks down slowly out of sight. It is as if you have surprised the ancient gods in conclave in some unexpected magic place. The curtain is lifted, and the curtain falls, leaving you wondering if it has ever really been up at all.

I have had one such vision. I was spinning for pike one September day from a high wall into the pool below a mill, and my reel jammed, as is the way of spinning reels which have been put away for a long summer. The bait curled round like a boomerang, accomplishing a complete semicircle, and finally attached itself to one of the paddles of the water-wheel, far away on my left. I had with me an obliging Philistine, one who fished not neither did he spin, but who seemed only too pleased at all times to undo tangles, to row a boat, and to remove flies from the inaccessible square inch between the shoulder-blades whither they are blown by contrary winds. This *rara avis*, therefore, now leaped over a large and spiky fence, negotiated a narrow plank, and finally reached the wheel to release my spinner. Suddenly he looked over the wheel into the deep narrow channel below it, and turned to me with a mighty bellow of joy. "Fish!" he said. "Enormous ones! Come and catch them!"

I know the uninitiated conception of "enormous"; and the railings were tall and spiky. So I was cautious. "What kind?" I asked.

"Obviously pike," said he, after consideration.

Therefore I climbed; and I got to the wheel just in time to see the last of them scattering before the shadow of the Philistine: whopping great torpedoes, that made a wave like a boat's wash as they fled from the insults which had been offered them. Chub, they were, and seven pounds each I'll give my oath; and even the Philistine nearly wept to see them go, for he had thought that big fish came only out of the sea.

To capture monsters such as these there have been various strange things devised, all of them sacrilegious, but some very successful. The fly-spoon is one, good both for chub and perch in heavy water, but abominable to my mind, because to cast it heavy tackle is required and a stiff and awkward rod. Without scales or feathers, it is neither fish nor fowl, nor even good red herring; but a sort of cross between all three. Another very ingenious way to catch big chub is to cast into likely spots, in the stillest of still dawns, a large imitation beetle, sinking it well and drawing it in jerks through mid-water. To the beetle's hook four or five gentles are attached, in order to convey the impression that the creature's "innards" have been squashed out of him in a most appetising manner. . . .

Personally I shall stick to my dry fly and pray for another brace of 3-pounders, rather than insult the immortals thus. It savours of offering up offal to the gods as a burnt sacrifice. . . . And so I advise you to let them be, the big fellows, the long mysterious shapes beneath the water-wheel, content merely to put a perky soldier-palmer (not too big) above their aristocratic noses in the hope that some miracle will bring one of them up to it and you may kill him in fair battle, without dishonour either to the slayer or to the slain.

And thus you will be able to look the purist straight in the eyes, when next he catches you on your way down to the river with your old greenheart that has a glorious kink in it all in honourable memory of the chub; and you can pass the fellow by light-heartedly, conscious of rectitude, and get on with the business of rowing your little boat along between the marching willows, into the dawn or into the sunset; and may you see many a big nose poked up at your fly, and hear many a good "plop" as the nose goes down, sounding out like a challenge to all purists among the summer silences.

CHAPTER X

by

H. D. Turing

BLACK BASS

EVER since Dr. Henshall pronounced his famous dictum that the black bass was "inch for inch and pound for pound the gamest fish that swims," American writers have outdone the lexicographers in their hunt for adjectives to describe the glories of fishing for the small-mouth bass. Authors have worked themselves into a very frenzy of delirium which leaves the reader gasping, and, like all such excrescences, creates in aftermath a certain feeling of opposition. "No, sir. We have no small-featured fish in this country–thank God!" perhaps sufficiently expresses the feelings of many anglers who have met the species only between columns of advertising matter in imported magazines. Not that *Micropterus dolomieu*, to give it its scientific name, really has a small mouth, except in comparison with *M. salmoides*. The difference is not more marked than in those of salmon and trout. But the small-mouth bass has become, for angling purposes, the American National Fish, and there is, in fact, some excuse for enthusiasm.

Bass in America must be, nowadays, almost as widely distributed as are chub in this country, and they grow to as great a size without acquiring that distressingly suspicious nature which makes fishing for them too much a matter of prostration and other undignified postures for anglers past their first youth. Moreover, the black bass is good eating, as good as perch, and no one who has tried perch from a clear-water stream will need a better recommendation than that. I have a secret conviction that this question of table qualities has more to do with our outlook on angling than most of us are prepared to admit.

What, I wonder, would be the annual value of some of our coarse-fishing rivers if chub were as welcome on the table as they are on the hook? If we can ever replace chub with bass we may witness an interesting change in the general outlook on coarse fishing.

There was a time when such a project did not seem so very distant. It is over thirty years ago that Alfred Jardine wrote of the black bass that they now "rank among our best for their sport-giving and superior edible qualifications." He was referring mainly, in all probability, to the fish imported by the Marquis of Exeter in the nineties, which were put into a lake at Burleigh Park, and a few years later were reported as having grown, some of them, to 6 or 8 pounds.

The weight, perhaps, is to be taken as "angler's reckoning"–they were the "small-mouth" variety which rarely exceeds 5 pounds, and there does not seem to be any record of fish of such weight being actually caught over here. But fish planted in new waters, before Nature has established her balance, do grow to an abnormal size in favourable conditions, so possibly the suspicion of inflated estimates is not justified. Anyhow, the fish grew and thrived, and, what is more, they spawned, for the Marquis wrote, from personal observation, a very good account of the spawning operations for the National Fish Cultural Association, and described how the eggs are laid in a sort of nest on the bottom, and the fry protected by the parent fish until they are able to fend for themselves.

What has happened to them? They were not the only consignment brought to this country by any means. As long ago as 1878 a Scotsman (Mr. Begg) residing in Toronto brought over a batch of fry, some of which went to a lake at Eynsham Hall near Oxford, and some to Dunrobin Castle in Scotland, the seat of the Duke of Sutherland. In view of the success of the earlier experiments, it seems certain that other importations were made. Jardine speaks of them as an established species in his time, but where can one get bass fishing in this country today?

A year or two ago I had hopes, great hopes, that before long bass would be acclimatised in the Broads. The Norfolk Fishery Board obtained some fry and planted them in what appeared to be a suitable lake. It was privately owned and practically never fished, an important point in a new essay, for it avoids losses among immature fish which are sure to be attracted by baits intended for other species. The water held good store of small Cyprinidæ, which might reasonably be expected to provide satisfactory rations for the newcomers. For the first two years all went well. Then came a change of ownership, and in the interregnum a local inhabitant obtained casual leave to fish the lake. He is reported to have caught "a number of strange fish," and no doubt their "superior edible qualifications" were noted with due, if inarticulate, appreciation round the family table. So at the moment it looks as if any immediate hopes of black bass fishing had been interred in a Norfolk cottage.

Apart from such accidents, it is very difficult to account for the almost complete failure to acclimatise bass over here. They seem to thrive quite satisfactorily in their early stages; it is when they are put into fishing waters with a free range that they disappear. It may be that lack of suitable conditions for spawning has something to do with it. Recently Mr. F. G. Richmond put forward the theory that the water in English lakes and rivers is not warm enough for bass to spawn in, and I am inclined to think he may have put his finger on the root of the trouble. Most fish seem unable to rid themselves of their eggs unless proper spawning facilities are available, and die if they become egg-bound.

Such "facilities," it is true, are generally mechanical in their action. Salmon and trout require suitable gravel, carp suitable weed. The mechanical factor for bass is probably debris—waterlogged twigs for example, of which there must be plenty in most of our lakes—but insufficient warmth in the water may be an equally effective barrier. Certainly the fry want warmth. This was shown effectively in a shipment of fry that was sent to South Africa recently. The consignment was sent off with a supply of food sufficient, according to the rate of feeding before despatch, to last the voyage. Directly the ship got into warmer latitudes the fry fed so vigorously that a further supply had to be obtained at Marseilles, since it was evident that the amount carried would be quite insufficient to last the voyage with the enhanced appetites which the warmer conditions engendered.

It seems curious that, in a mild climate like England, the water should not be warm enough, considering the severe conditions which exist in Eastern Canada where the fish is indigenous, and where the waters it inhabits are often ice-bound for four or five months of the year. But, in fact, the inhabited part of the country is much further south than we are, and it is probable that the summer temperature of the water is higher. This matter of temperature may possibly account for the success of the earlier experiments here. About once in a decade we are treated to a summer like that of 1929, when shallows must be many degrees above their normal temperature. Such a summer arriving opportunely, just when the young fish had reached maturity, might enable them to carry on for a generation before the English climate wiped them out.

But all the earlier experiments seem to have been made with the small-mouth variety. Has anyone tried the large-mouth? It may be that the large-mouth, whose natural habitat is still further south, might prove an even worse coloniser than the small, but it is accustomed to more equable, if warmer, conditions, and moreover it is accustomed to weed. Anyone who has fished both here and in Canada must have been struck with the wealth of weed which our waters contain in comparison with those where the small-mouth bass flourishes. Has this superabundance of weed any effect on the fish? I do not know; but, apart from the range of temperature, it is the only obvious difference to a fisherman. Discussion, even heated discussion, often arises, in places where both fish are available, on the respective merits of bass and trout fishing as a sport. The two fish are so entirely different in their habits, except perhaps in certain rivers, that comparison seems hardly possible. Where it is a question of stocking the case is otherwise. Trout and bass cannot be put in the same water with any chance of success–it must be one or the other. The bass, if they thrive at all, will inevitably destroy the trout. I knew a lake once, holding a good head of *fontinalis*, in which small bass suddenly appeared. Inquiry unearthed a tragic history of a consignment of fingerling bass intended for another water; a pause for refreshment at a village; a subsequent, and consequent, uncertainty about the route; and the heaven-sent appearance of a lake in which a weary carter might rid himself of an aching head and a burden of fish at the same time.

Later, the lake provided some excellent bass fishing, but the trout were no more, except for a remnant which could be caught on an occasional day. From their dark colour it was evident they had taken refuge somewhere in inaccessible depths.

But there is no reason why a trout fisherman should not also be a bass fisherman. Indeed, the two species fit very well into the fly-fisher's season. Bass come in just when the mayfly is well over, the end of June or beginning of July, at a time when trout, except in a few favoured streams, are taking their mid-season siesta. There is a certain flatness about trout fishing for awhile after the mayfly season. Even if one has access to a stream where the fly is unknown and the fish feed on as usual, the recollection of those mighty "plops" makes smaller rings seem trifles. Bass fishing is a fine medicine for the summer of our discontent.

To enjoy it to the full, at least in lakes, the fishing should be done from a canoe. I seem to hear a muttered objection that no one can enjoy any kind of fishing while performing a balancing feat on a craft that feels like an insecurely slung hammock. It is true that some ease in a canoe is best acquired before attempting to fish from one; but the feeling that the only safe position is a reclining one on the bottom, or at best an attitude of prayer with both hands grasping the gunwales, soon passes, and one can sit and cast as comfortably from the thwart seat of a canoe as from the solid deal of the tubbiest of boats. Did I possess a lake containing bass, my first care would be to install a Canadian canoe on its banks.

A canoe, of course, implies also a gillie to do the paddling. An attempt to fish single-handed from a canoe, except in the most breathless of calms, is not likely to be repeated. If you succeed in making one effective cast in an hour you may consider that the gods are kind. Even the most carefully balanced canoe, with a sack of sand of just the right weight in the bow, drifts so rapidly that long before line has been extended you will find yourself 20 yards from your objective.

But with an expert paddler it is the most delightful form of bass fishing. The craft steals forward towards the bank in almost complete silence, except for the gentle hollow ripple against her bow, and the little hissing drip of the paddle as it goes forward for the swaying urge of another stroke. Bass of any size seldom feed in the open, unless there is an uprising shelf of rock. Small fry of a quarter to half a pound, yearlings probably from the previous summer's hatching, may be found on the shallows, but fish of substantial weight must be sought along the banks where the water is deep and overhung.

In Canada the shore line of most bass lakes has plenty of cover, both on the bank and in the water. Waterlogged timbers from some former "log run" have drifted to the side, and winter gales have felled many a forest tree which once held fast the bank. Driftweed has made a platform for frogs among the branches, and it is in the shade of this fallen debris that a good fish is likely to be found. I have never been able to decide whether the fish lie doggo waiting for the many chance morsels which such a larder provides, or whether they cruise along the shore line in the deep water and rise quickly to seize their prey. Bass show a nervous irritability which makes one think that a waiting game must be altogether foreign to their nature, and they grow so rapidly that an active pursuit of food would seem necessary to supply their need. But their method of taking a fly in such places bears far more resemblance to a fish lying in wait than to a forager which sights and pursues its prey from afar.

It is in this, very largely, that the attraction of the sport lies. There is none of that persistent casting into a waste of water which a drift across a lake after trout entails–and when the fish are not rising it can be a weariness indeed. The cast for a bass is made as close in to shore as possible, or just alongside a log, or in any place where there is cover for a fish, and worked slowly out. There is in it much the same spirit of adventure as in the exploration of an upland trout-stream, where every bend may reveal a pool or ripple which will add measurably to the basket.

As a rule the fish takes the fly with a rush, almost immediately it touches the water. Seldom have I known a fly to be seized after more than a yard or two of line has been recovered. If the water is calm and the light right, the whole process can be seen. I must confess to a weakness for fishing in a calm. The fly can be cast so neatly into some little bay among the floating debris, which a heavy ripple usually prevents; and there is a special joy in seeing that green streak suddenly materialise from the shadows as the line comes taut.

It has seemed to me, too, that bass, when hooked, leap more persistently in calm water; but that may be only imagination, and I am never quite sure whether this terrifying performance is to be placed to the credit or debit side of the account. Once the fish is in the boat, of course, it becomes the leading *motif* in the song of triumph, but in progress its only fitting accompaniment is deep Ionian curses.

One of my most vivid recollections is of a fish of about 2½ pounds which made seven consecutive leaps like the arches of an aerial bridge in a complete semicircle round the boat, forming a series of momentary rainbows across the water. But that is not typical of the fish's leap. Normally it jumps straight into the air, shaking itself viciously as it does so, for all the world like a terrier dealing faithfully with its first rat.

I doubt, though, whether a calm day is often profitable. My best fish have nearly always been caught when there was a fairly heavy swell on the water, which makes casting near obstructions more difficult. Fortunately bass seem to rely more upon their strength and acrobatic ability than upon cunning to effect their escape. Chub hooked in such places would be round a sunken log in no time, but bass usually elect to fight in the open. One of the best fish I ever caught, an ounce or two under 4 pounds, could have got free fifty times in the fifteen minutes or so it took me to land it. I was by myself in a clumsy, flat-bottomed boat in the early morning with an on-shore breeze just getting up when I hooked it under a fallen spruce. The bank was littered with half-submerged timber, and as the boat drifted with the wind I thought every moment it would become entangled in the maze of branches which lined the shore. Not once, but half a dozen times, the fish pulled the boat clear at a critical moment, and was finally scooped into the net just as a heavy bump told me we had gone aground.

For this kind of fishing I think it is a mistake to use too light a rod. A 10-foot 6-inch split cane weighing 9 or 10 ounces is the kind of weapon which suits the fishing–in fact, a mayfly rod, line, and cast, such as would be suitable for the Kennet or Avon, does very well. It is often necessary to cast a long line across the wind, though if the banks are timbered, a condition which seems to suit bass, a head wind of any force has seldom to be negotiated. Flies are, of course, of the "impressionist" variety. Most of the outrageous creations which pass as "lures" will catch fish, but I doubt if they have any special merit over the more usual type of large fly. Actually bass, except when they are small, do not feed on insects to any considerable extent, and a silver-bodied fly representing some kind of small fish is probably as good as any. Curiously enough, however, I could never get fish on an Alexandra, which one would have supposed ideal for the purpose. Whatever dressing is used, the fly should sink quickly.

The fly with which I have had most success is rather like a Blagdon March Brown with large green wings. Probably it was taken for a frog, of which bass seem to be inordinately fond. A fly tied so as to resemble a frog's shape might well prove very killing. The only successful fly belonging to the not-very-exact imitation class was a home-made affair with a dark mohair body and a large mallard hackle laid along the length of the hook. When the strands of the feather were divided into "legs" with the tying silk, it faintly resembled the larva of a dragon-fly, and proved useful later in the season over rocky reefs.

Bass in rivers at first sight seem to have very different habits from those in lakes. They show a decided preference for the type of stream one associates with salmon—the larger type of salmon river such as the Welsh Dee. A well-known American angler, in writing of his visit to this country a few years ago, intimated that he thought the Wye would make an excellent river for bass. The effect of the pronouncement over here may be imagined. It is believed that the banks of the river caved in in some parts after the suggestion appeared in print. But he was right. The Wye is just the kind of river bass would select were they given a choice, and one cannot help a certain sympathy for their selection. A movement to restock the Wye Valley with a new species of angler would have many supporters—among the new species.

In flowing water it is rarely much use fishing for bass in the long, quiet reaches, unless the bed and banks are decidedly rocky. The pool at the tail of a riffle or small waterfall is the most likely place. It is a case of downstream fishing. "Down and across," after the manner of working a salmon fly, will take fish; but a more attractive way is to flick a fly, with some little slack line, into a run and let the water wash the fly down into the pool below. The slack line is necessary to allow the fly to be carried into the undertow. It is quite likely that many fish are missed, for a rise is not felt until the slack line is being gathered in, but it generally accounts for the best fish. Wandering, or if accuracy is demanded stumbling, down the rocky bed of a stream and fishing a short line in every stickle that has a pool at its foot can be a very attractive method of fishing.

I have tried sometimes to picture to myself the probable "lies" of bass, should they be successfully acclimatised in some of our coarse-fishing rivers—the Hampshire Avon, for example, or the Great Ouse—but I confess they are difficult to visualise. Long trailing weed and black bass fishing somehow will not take their right perspective in the picture—and it is in such rivers that they would (or perhaps one should say might) be most useful. A dangerous experiment? Possibly; but I am inclined to think the danger of black bass consuming all the other species is rather overrated. In rivers a voracious fish seldom seems able to establish an ascendancy over its more helpless neighbours, possibly because its voracity leads it more readily to the anglers' creel. It is fish like chub, which starve their neighbours out, that do the real damage—and bass might prove a good antidote to the undue increase of chub.

But, rivers apart, there are surely many waters in England where black bass could be planted with some chance of success. "Bass fishing in our time" would be no bad slogan for an energetic fishing club.

CHAPTER XI

by

A. F. Bell

THE FLY-ROD IN THE SEA

NOT long ago I asked a çi-devant fly-fisherman, too afflicted with gout at that time to indulge in his sport, whether he had ever thought of fishing in the sea. His only reply was a snort worthy of a buffalo, while his complexion threatened apoplexy. Perceiving that he was one of those "old timers" toiling painfully miles (or is it years?) behind the times, to whom sea fishing means merely a pound of lead and an ounce of dab, I thought it best to change the subject. Later when he was grumbling at the pollution of our rivers and the ever-growing expense and scarcity of good trout and salmon waters, I was tempted to return to the attack. Discretion, synonymous in this case with sheer cowardice, once more deterred me. Now, however, I can put my case for the fly-rod in salt water, without fear of personal injury, into a book which he and many like him will be sure to read. He and they will be surprised, perhaps, to know that many sea anglers have long since converted their former sea rods into clothes props and their lines into blind cords, and today go fishing in the sea with a fly-rod, and a fly-rod only.

There are really two headings under which we had better consider the subject: (1) Fly-fishing in the sea, and (2) Drift-line fishing with bait and a fly-rod.

In dealing with fly-fishing in the sea it will be best, perhaps, to look first at the gloomy side of the picture. Obviously it is not much use to "search for haddocks' eyes among the heather bright," whatever the ancient man in *Alice through the Looking-Glass* may have said to the contrary, and it is equally futile to go fly-fishing in the sea unless a place is chosen where the right kinds of fish are in the habit of feeding on the surface or of pursuing the britt and other small fry into shallow inlets or bays. In short, a very large proportion of the British coast is useless for fly-fishing in the sea, either because the surface-feeding fish such as the coalfish, pollack, bass, mackerel, and garfish are not p resent or because they confine themselves to deep water. On the other hand, if this fact is realised, it is not difficult to choose a place where fly-fishing in the sea *can* be enjoyed, and there are infinite possibilities about the sport which have not been explored to the full.

Let us consider those places on the east coast of England which are already famous for the sport. The best known are perhaps Filey Brig, Hayburn Wyke, and Cloughton Wyke in Yorkshire.

Filey Brig is a somewhat sinister reef of rocks running out perhaps half a mile into the sea, and round and about it large numbers of billet (pollack and coalfish) and mackerel are wont to feed freely near the surface throughout the late summer months. On this reef large numbers of anglers may be observed casting their flies into the ocean, whence they collect some surprisingly good baskets, and not infrequently surprisingly wet clothes into the bargain. The Brig, though normally safe enough, is not always free from danger, and there are cases of anglers finding themselves unexpectedly wallowing among their quarry either through the agency of a slippery piece of seaweed (unpleasant) or an inordinately big wave (diabolical). It is a reef that wants knowing, and the question of tides should be studied with some care.

Most anglers use a salmon rod of from 14 to 17 feet in length (either whole cane or greenheart), a checked salmon reel, and a waterproofed line. The cast is generally made of salmon gut or gut substitute with three sea flies attached.

The word "fly," of course, is not strictly accurate, for although the monstrosities used in the sea are tied much in the same way as flies, they are, in fact, imitations of small fish. There are numerous excellent sea flies on the market, and there is not much to choose between most of them, since the sea fish, when on the feed, do not show the nice discrimination of the Test trout. Perhaps the most popular patterns for the Brig are Percy Wadham's celluloid-bodied flies in green and silver with white wings. Strips of sole or gurnard skin are often used instead of the white feather. There are also some rather primitive though killing patterns compounded chiefly of white rubber tubing or white leather.

That the sport is at times first class is shown by a letter from a friend which I have before me. He writes as follows: "At times the sport is excellent but very uncertain. Big coalfish and pollack are taken, with many mackerel and gurnard, and often a good codling. Once or twice I have known a salmon taken here, but this is a very rare occurrence. Personally I have caught 90 pounds (estimate, most of the fish being returned to the sea alive) of pollack, averaging 4 pounds each, in an afternoon, and I have seen catches of upwards of 200 mackerel taken in the same space of time. The largest fish I have killed on the fly is a pollack of 10 pounds and a cod of 9 pounds. My wife has killed a 12-pound pollack. Larger fish are frequently hooked, but seldom landed, since it is difficult to hold them out of the adjacent weed beds."

An uncle of my own who at one time fished fairly regularly from Filey Brig, and who, by the way, favoured a split-cane trout rod, used to tell the story of how, fishing with three flies, he landed simultaneously a coalfish, a mackerel, and a Skye Terrier dog (the last-named having, of course, dived in after the first two). Personally, I was always a little disappointed that he did not round off the story with a gigantic wave precipitating the whole "boiling," uncle and all, into the ocean.

Speaking of trout rods, I have always found that the most satisfactory and delightful rod to use for all types of fly-fishing in the sea is a 12-foot split-cane trout or sea-trout rod. It can be wielded with one hand (wrist strength permitting) and will assure the maximum amount of sport.

That the dividing line between fly-fishing proper and spinning is a very narrow one is shown by the methods sometimes adopted at Scarborough. Seven or eight plain white flies are attached to a long cast at intervals of a few inches apart. A light lead is fastened to the head of the cast and another smaller piece of lead to the tail. The whole contraption is lowered into the water and worked with a sink-and-draw motion close along the pier side. This method often accounts for big catches of coalfish and an occasional mackerel or cod. The fly used is a narrow white feather from a duck's wing lashed to any make of hook. How in the world the fish can mistake the formidable array for anything subaquatic, unless it be a marine flag day, will always remain a mystery.

While on the subject of Scarborough it might be of interest to mention that sport can be had at "The Lady's Dock," a rocky place at the north end of the Marine Drive, and at the first point on the south (about 1 mile from the town) where two little bays formed by the quarrying of stone for pier building provide inlets into which the billet and mackerel pursue their prey.

At Cloughton Wyke and Hayburn Wyke the methods of angling are crude and primitive, and the anglers are chiefly farm-hands and labourers. These worthies use long bamboos with a short tight line attached to the top and a white fly of the rough-and-ready type previously mentioned. Considering that even on this tackle plenty of fish are caught, what a wonderful opportunity for the expert fly-fisher!

The fact that a great deal of fly-fishing is done on the east coast does not mean that there are no other places equally good. For instance, some of the sea lochs on the west of Scotland are wonderful places for coalfish.

I had an amusing experience once when salmon fishing near Loch Inchard (top north-west corner of Scotland). One evening I happened to notice a lot of fish "boiling" in the sea loch and promptly rushed for a sea-trout rod. In the absence of sea flies I put up a Durham Ranger and started casting among the fish, which on closer inspection proved to be coalfish. They were not in the least shy, and in half an hour I had beached eight or nine fish up to about 4 pounds, and an excellent fight the bigger ones put up. The conclusion of the sport coincided with the appearance of a fat seal, whose intrusion the coalfish seemed to resent; anyway, they departed with great promptitude.

That it is possible to catch very large coalfish on the west coasts of both Scotland and Ireland there can be no doubt, and I am sure that with the aid of a boat some really startling catches could be achieved.

Perhaps the most delightful sea fish which can be made to surrender to the flyfisher's wiles is the bass. Unfortunately he is an uncertain customer and is not always to be found on the feed. Generally speaking, a boat is needed for bass fishing, and only the small or "school" bass will be taken on the fly. If an angler has the good fortune to find the young bass and his brothers and sisters breaking after britt, and can get within casting distance, the sport will be memorable; for even a small bass will fight like a tiger on fly tackle. Bass usually go in for surface feeding in the neighbourhood of sandbanks or in shoal water, and such places should be sought by the would-be bass fly-fisher. The Isle of Wight is excellent in this way, and many good bags of bass have been made in the neighbourhood of the forts off that island.

Few people know that the best fly-fishing for bass that the British Isles can provide is to be had round the Eddystone Lighthouse. At almost all states of tide a huge shoal of bass (and not all small ones) can be found breaking close up to the Eddystone, and there is a very expert angler living at Looe who has caught not a few of them.

Of course the weather must be fine, for otherwise it is highly unsafe to approach too close to that sinister rock. I believe when it is very calm certain intrepid anglers have landed on the rock itself and have learned the true magnificence of fly-fishing in the sea. I once visited the Eddystone myself, but, as invariably happens when I sally forth with great expectations, the wind got up from the south-west and before long the cross seas became somewhat aweinspiring. With the peculiar tides at the Eddystone, it is nothing unusual to see four waves approaching simultaneously from four different directions so that the unhappy boat knows not whether to pitch or roll or simply give up the unequal struggle and turn over on its face. Mine fortunately was more courageous. Anyway, fly-fishing for bass would have been about as useful as roller-skating on the Rocky Mountains. I hope some day to try the Eddystone again.

At many places along the coast of Wales there is good bass fishing, and when business takes you to Llandudno and other parts of the Principality you might do worse than include a fly-rod in your luggage.

Plate No. 2

One more note about bass fishing: if you value your life don't take a novice fly-fishing in a small boat; for generally speaking the large bass fly will be far more frequently embedded in some part of your anatomy (his doesn't matter) than it will be in the mouth of a bass. Let him practise by himself or with a horny-skinned and blasphemous boatman.

To return for the moment to the possibilities of fly-fishing in the sea, I can well remember an occasion when I was bottom fishing from an anchored boat off Cornwall. The sea was very calm, and I noticed a school of mackerel breaking within reasonable reach of the boat. I had a fly-rod aboard, and to this I affixed a somewhat weighty sea reel, mounted a trout cast, and then wondered what to do for a fly. By a kindly dispensation of providence I found a small blue and silver sea-trout fly of uncertain age and pattern fixed in my hat-band. Perspiring freely in the hot sun, I cast energetically among the mackerel, which always seemed a yard or two further away than was absolutely convenient. To my surprise I caught three, and should probably have landed a fourth and the biggest had not a large conger fastened itself to my bottom tackle, which was fishing by itself. The line, by some mysterious process known only to itself and its relations, had taken a turn round the handle of the reel and the rod was proceeding quietly overboard when I grabbed it with my left hand. Thereupon I found myself playing a mackerel on light fly tackle to starboard and a large conger (not on fly tackle) to port. This sort of thing might have continued indefinitely had not the mackerel taken a turn round the anchor rope and disappeared with my only fly, while the conger had gone firmly to ground, where he ultimately remained with my hook.

I am sure from that experience that there are times when mackerel can be caught in the open sea on fly, but I do not think they often come within range.

There can be no question that a man of imagination and of an inventive turn of mind might achieve some remarkable results were he to devote time and thought to this delightful subject. The two following incidents illustrate my point.

A friend of mine was stationed at Shoeburyness, and he observed during his evening constitutional that there were a number of smallish fish moving about among the surface weed close to the shore. He rigged up a sorry-looking white fly and tried casting among these fish. To his intense amusement he caught some—red mullet!

Again yet another friend was fishing off Cornwall for big bottom mackerel (not with a fly), and was casting pilchard oil and chopped mackerel into the water as ground bait. Shortly he noticed, to his surprise, a number of large mackerel coming up in the clear water and taking the chopped mackerel quite close to the surface. This fairly ordinary occurrence opens up the question of how far it might be possible to attract the fish to the surface and then take them with a fly.

The fly-fisher in the sea must be an opportunist, and it is a matter for regret that a fly-rod cannot be carried about in the waistcoat pocket. It happens always to be hanging up in the hall just when the mackerel have come into the harbour.

So far I have treated my subject from a somewhat insular point of view, and it is clear that before turning our attention to drift-line fishing a word must be said on the possibilities of fly-fishing in foreign seas.

Since these latter are in much the same ratio to British possibilities as the Bank of England is to the child's money-box, it can be seen that to do full justice to the question it would be necessary to write a book and not a mere chapter. It must be admitted, on the other hand, that very few people, in very few places, have tried to catch foreign fish on a fly, and that the limits of the field for exploration are the limits also of this planet.

That the tarpon can be taken on a fly is well known, and since this is a glorious and sporting fish, it may be worth seeing what methods are employed in his capture. The tarpon frequently runs into estuaries and inlets of various kinds, and it is in such places that he may be taken on the fly. A fascinating account by Mr. William Markham, who lives in the neighbourhood of the famous Gatun Dam on the Panama Canal, gives a vivid description of the sport. After describing how the shrimps and small fish percolate through the hydro-electric plant and through spillway gates into the Chagres River estuary, and how the tarpon apparently congregate to welcome such gifts as the gods of the dam have to offer them, he portrays the angler standing on a slippery rock at dawn, casting his large fly into what he calls a "pocket." His description of the ensuing battle, which begins at the moment when the tarpon hits the fly "with the force of a locomotive," fills one with enthusiasm. It appears that the odds are ten to one on the tarpon, and yet such sportsmen are these Panama anglers that when at length the ten-to-one chance in the shape of a 55-pounder is safely landed, it is returned to the water. Take heed, ye slaughterers of 6-inch trout!

Another peep into the joys of foreign fly-fishing is provided by a member of the British Sea Anglers' Society, writing from that distant and turbulent land, China. This is his description of a day's bass fishing with the fly in Chinese waters.

"At breakfast on this last morning the family had, in the way that families have, expressed their opinion of my fishing in good set terms: it was merely a waste of time, and I would be well advised to pack up the rod and join in their bathing picnic. I was forced to admit–to myself, of course, not to them–that their remarks were not without reason. Was the fishing really hopeless? Or should I have one more try? As I pondered the point I remembered the story of the Chinese sage famed in days of old for fishing without a hook. He, so the tale went, always weighed in with the heaviest creel because the fish, touched by his kindness, insisted on being caught by him even if they had to hang on to his line with their teeth. I was not a sage—that at least had been made clear at breakfast—but could not something be done even by me to win over fortune to my side? Suppose I left the landing-net behind to tempt Providence into sending a fish and perhaps a big one at that? There and then I decided to try it. . . . I made my way to Fish-hook Point, where lay the pools fished without success for two long days. . . . I moved from place to place, casting as I went, in the hope of getting a rise. At last I decided to go home, and would have done so had I not, in the very moment of resignation, caught sight of a line of rocks 30 yards out to sea. If I can get out there, I told myself, I may yet get a fish, and dropping off the point out I swam, and gained the biggest rock, rod in hand, without mishap other than a few insignificant scratches. Once on top a rapid survey revealed a deep gap between the rocks through which the sea was pouring deep and smooth. The very place for bass if there were any. Into this I cast, and at the third attempt there was a swirl, and I struck and hooked my first bass, not a large fish as bass go, barely 2 pounds as it turned out, but my very first—and please remember I was fishing with a light trout rod, a thin cast, and no landing-net, and the fish was fighting gamely. In no circumstances could I afford to lose it, for the family lacked faith where fishing was concerned, and would, I knew quite well, regard it as a fish of the imagination unless actually produced for their inspection. Torn by hope and fear, therefore, I slowly worked my bass (I already thought of it as *my* bass) round the rock to a sloping ledge, brought it in on the crest of a wave, and fell upon it before it could escape. It was mine at last, but it had yet to be killed, and there was nothing in sight except a stone on a rock some ten yards off. Now I was not prepared to risk the loss of my first, possibly my last, bass by swimming across to the rock with it in my hands, but something had to be done, and done quickly. . . . It was a very isolated spot, and so an essential garment was hurriedly slipped off and into "them" went the bass, secured with a few deft turns to hold it until I returned. One tap with the stone was sufficient, and having placed it with care in a niche of the rock I returned with joy in my heart to the fishing. Soon another bass was hooked and landed, and then another and another, until eleven all of the same size lay side by side on the rock. . . . My sacrifice had been accepted by fortune."

A South American writer tells of catching jack, snook, bone fish, and even red snappers on the fly. So here is a glimpse of those vast and delightful possibilities to which I am ever referring; and when you think of all the seas, all the coasts, all the estuaries in the world, and of all the myriads of different fish known to science, you will perhaps be able to visualise some of the opportunities that lie in wait for the pioneer fly-fisher.

Now at last we come to part two of my subject—namely, drift-line fishing with a fly-rod. Inasmuch as this sport has been very fully dealt with by other writers (an excellent description is contained in Mr. F. D. Holcombe's book, *Modern Sea Angling*), I do not propose to give more than a very brief outline of it here. That it can provide greater enjoyment than almost any other form of bait-fishing is well known among the modern generation of sea anglers, and it is well worthy of the attention of the fly-fisherman when he happens to be holiday-making with his family by the sea. Again the principal fish to be caught are mackerel, pollack, coalfish, bass, and garfish. Of these perhaps the most satisfactory to fish for with a trout fly-rod are the big bottom mackerel to be found off the Cornish coast. The procedure is fairly simple. Choose a "mark" where the mackerel are known to feed and where there is not too much tide—anchor the boat and mount a trout fly-rod (split cane for preference)—attach a small wooden reel with 50 yards of silk line dressed with animal fat, and add a lake-trout gut cast (gut substitute will do quite well) and a fairly long-shanked hook. If there is little or no tide leave all lead in the bag and trust to your swivel, which, incidentally, I omitted to mention, to take the line down. Plumb the depth much as the roach angler would do, and then mark the depth by attaching a piece of coloured silk to the line. After removing the plummet, bait the hook with a small strip or "last" of fresh mackerel and pay out the line until the coloured silk mark is touching the water. If there is a gentle tide running the line will be streaming out with the bait about a fathom from the bottom, and if the tide strengthens it is only necessary to pay out more line. The big Cornish mackerel average from $1\frac{1}{2}$ pounds to 2 pounds, and when you have driven home the hook into a 2-pounder the battle must be experienced to be believed. A terrific fighter, the mackerel will keep your rod bent in a complete arc and your reel screaming for the best part of a quarter of an hour; he will circle the boat and make run after run; and even when you have him beaten it is necessary to drag him, still fighting, into the landing-net. One of the best places in the world to enjoy this big mackerel fishing is a submerged reef called the Gwingeas Rocks, off Megavissey, and there mackerel up to nearly 3 pounds in weight have been caught. Only last year, fishing in this manner in the harbour mouth at Fowey, my wife and I took thirty mackerel of from 1 pound to 2 pounds in an afternoon, and it can be imagined that both rods were bent double nearly all the time. It adds greatly to the gaiety of nations if a big pollack takes a fancy to the bait, and the capture of a

10-pounder on a trout fly-rod is so exciting that it is impossible to describe unless one sprinkles the paper with a regular volley of superlatives.

If pollack are the aim and object of the expedition it is best really to employ a grilse rod, as it is necessary as a rule to fish in somewhat deeper water and to use about an ounce of lead (a Jardine spiral lead is the most satisfactory); otherwise the process is practically identical except that the strip of mackerel should be cut much longer. The first rush of a pollack for the weeds is calculated to fill the most blasé angler with excitement, especially when he is using this light tackle.

A fly-rod is the ideal weapon, too, for bass fishing. The procedure generally differs from mackerel fishing in that live prawns and sand eels are the best baits and a small float is often a *sine qua non*.

Last of all we come to the black bream, a fish which has received no previous mention in this chapter. His habits are rather strange in that he appears off a very small stretch of our coast, and then only for one month in the year. His happy hunting-grounds extend, roughly, from Brighton to Bognor, and he times his appearance to coincide almost exactly with that of the mayfly –namely, from May 15 to June 15. (I am not suggesting, of course, that he is interested in that insect!) He runs in weight from about $\frac{3}{4}$ pound to 3 pounds, and is one of the most sporting fighters to be found in the sea. Use the same tackle and methods for his capture as you would for mackerel, but substitute that somewhat offensive creature the lugworm for the strip of mackerel bait. The most important item in black bream fishing is perhaps the marking of the line, and since this fish feeds at varying depths it is an excellent plan to have different coloured silk marks for each of the first six fathoms of line; thus, if a bream is caught, the line can be paid out again to precisely the same depth.

I have said enough, perhaps, to show that there are forms of sea fishing worthy of the consideration of the trout fly-fisherman, and I hope a few of those who read this book will explore some of the possibilities which I have suggested.

It may be that one day we shall hear of Carnera catching a giant tunny on a 20-foot salmon fly-rod and a fly the size of a herring! Why not?

CHAPTER XII

with

Mr. Arthur N. Gilbey

A TALK ABOUT IT

[In the dialogue which follows, Mr. Gilbey is Piscator and Venator is a humble disciple who called upon him to try to wheedle the material for a chapter out of one who (like that other great dry-fly man Marryatt) has so far been silent in print.]

VENATOR: I have been staring in rapt silence at J. M. W. Turner's fishing-rod, in the case over your head; and I have been thinking that this room must be full of the friendly ghosts of "gentle anglers," it has so many relics of them.... I should like to hear about some of them, if I may. But perhaps it would be convenient to start by telling me about the Houghton Club, which I believe is the oldest fishing club in this country?

PISCATOR: I think it is; though lately the *Angler's News* seems to have unearthed two older ones. I should be interested to know if they have continuous records. The Longstock Club—whose water was just above Stockbridge—was founded in the latter part of the seventeenth century, but has been de-

S

funct for some years. Towards the end of its existence there were only four members. Indeed, I seem to have heard talk of a club that possessed but one, who performed of necessity the offices of president, honorary secretary, treasurer, and committee, all at once!

VENATOR: In that sense we are all of us clubs–even I, when I journey out after my trivial minnows. . . . I certainly think we must give the palm to the Houghton Club.

PISCATOR: Well, it was formed in 1822, and so has been in existence for 108 years. Curiously enough, in all that time it has had only four secretaries, and I have held that post for the last twenty-eight years. And our keeper, Lunn, has been with us for over forty years.

VENATOR: Can you account for the Club's unique position in the fishing world? Money could not insure it, I know. Perhaps there is some special virtue in antiquity; but first of all there must be some secret of good fellowship which has carried it through more than a century.

PISCATOR: Probably the "secret" is that we have very few rules to worry about. And we have only seventeen members, so we all know each other very well. And, no doubt, the river has something to do with it.

VENATOR: Of course. I suppose the Test is to the world of fishing what Lord's is to cricket, or St. Andrews to golf, or Aintree to steeplechasing. So your water at Stockbridge has the atmosphere of the finest dry-fly fishing on the finest river in the world. I wonder if it has changed much in a hundred years? Do you catch more fish than you used to do, or fewer?

PISCATOR: Oh, more; but that, I think, is chiefly because there are more to be caught. We stock the water well, but the fish grow wiser, I am sure. There was a time when, if you saw a fish rising in deep water, you could be certain that if you put your fly over him decently you would get a rise out of him and very likely catch him. But now you have not got that certainty; he may be too wise for you. He has been tried before. . . . Here are the old records of the Club. You see that in 1896 we killed only 260 trout, including 24 of 3 pounds or over. Jump a few years, and you find that in 1907 we had 972, averaging just over 2 lbs.

VENATOR: When you turned over the pages I noticed a curious entry, I think by a Mr. Penn. He had caught some grayling, and he had put them down with fine disgust:

> Horrid grayling.
> Filthy ditto.
> Beastly ditto.

So even as long ago as that they regarded grayling as a pest?

PISCATOR: Yes, and so do we now. It's amazing how quickly they breed in our water. Look, in 1896, we caught only 85; and now I have a letter in my pocket from a member who has been down several week-ends since the end of the trout season, with a friend, trying to thin them out, and he has had over 600, by fair fishing with fly. These will not appear in our records unless over $1\frac{1}{2}$ pounds, and actually very few of them are over that weight.

VENATOR: To return to trout—I wonder how much the methods we use to catch them have altered in the last century? For instance, has the display of rods at Stockbridge changed much in character during the last twenty years? Do members support the *reductio ad absurdum* of recent days, 6-foot and 7-foot rods?

PISCATOR: Of course the rods have changed; you have only to look at Turner's fly-rod to see that! Why, even when I first joined the Club some members were using double-handed rods! And Seymour Corkran and Martin-Smith used to blow with a natural mayfly, using a whole-cane rod of 20 feet; indeed, there was little serious fishing after the mayfly in those days. All that has changed; but none of our members use the very short rods—9 feet is about the shortest.

VENATOR: What size do you use yourself?

PISCATOR: I have two 10-foot rods—a "Halford Pattern" and a "Hardy's Itchen," which is rather stiffer than the Halford. Personally, I should not care to use anything much shorter.

VENATOR: Do you take the other shibboleths and new doctrines very seriously?

PISCATOR: About flies and so on? No, I can't say I do; though I use a nymph occasionally, so I'm not the old sort of purist. And I use hackle flies a great deal with success. But after all, in spite of new notions, as a great fisherman once said, "It's not the fly but the driver."

VENATOR: That was Marryatt, wasn't it?

PISCATOR: Yes. I remember him very well, and I think he was certainly one of the greatest anglers I have ever known. He would catch fish when nobody else could, and his casting was wonderful. He used to come down with a great bundle of rods—dozens of them—and great heavy gun-metal reels. But he taught me a lot. I remember that I was fishing with him one day, and there was a fish rising round the corner of a bush. I knew I couldn't reach it, so I asked Marryatt to show me how to do it. Flick-flick—and he'd risen it and hooked it: a most miraculous cast. Then he asked me to play it, saying it was really my fish; but I said no, he'd caught it and he must play it—whereupon he planted the spear of his rod in the ground and left it. So I picked up his rod and played his fish, and in the end I landed it. Marryatt was a great man.

VENATOR: Nowadays I suppose one has to fish very fine for Test trout?

PISCATOR: I'm not so sure about that. Personally I never use gut finer than

2x, though, of course, I choose that gut very carefully for transparency, etc. As a matter of fact, most of our members, I think, fish with 3x.

VENATOR: What in your view is the best time to catch Test trout nowadays –in the morning rise, or when there is no definite rise going on, or in the evening?

PISCATOR: That's difficult to say. It depends so much on the weather, and the hatch of fly, and other circumstances. One certain thing is that the evening rise seems to have gone off lately. We don't get so much fly as we used to do. One cause is that the weather is generally bad for the duns when they lay their eggs. I can tell you rather an interesting thing about the duns. Our keeper, Lunn, spotted it first. He found quantities of fly ova on the bottom of the punt which he was using for weed cutting. That interested him, and in the end he discovered that the duns like to lay their eggs on the underside of boarding, under the wooden bridges, and such like. That accounts for the fact that there is almost always a rising fish underneath a bridge–particularly a wooden bridge. So nowadays we put down special boards in the river, anchored in suitable places, for the duns to lay their eggs upon, and in this way the eggs are safer from their enemies and a good proportion are hatched out. One has to try to keep the caddis off the boards, though; otherwise they eat the duns' eggs.

VENATOR: It would be interesting to know what has been your most exciting adventure in fishing at Stockbridge. . . .

PISCATOR: Oh, that's difficult to remember! One has a good many in any day's fishing. Perhaps the most thrilling was the occasion in the mayfly time when I hooked two fish in succession, which both went down through a hatch in a weir. In each case all the line had to be taken off the reel, let down through the hatch-hole, and put through the rings again, while the fish was still on at the end of it. I got the first one out, which weighed over 3 pounds, but the second broke me, and he was the bigger fish. He must have been 20 yards above the weir when I hooked him, because I myself was standing above it, and he was a good way upstream of me. As soon as he felt my fly he came down in a great rush, as hard as he could, and before I knew where I was he had gone through. . . . And then there was an evening when I went out after dinner and caught eight fish before dusk; but I don't think I shall tell you about that.

VENATOR: Why not?

PISCATOR: Well, one doesn't particularly want to boast about great slaughters.

VENATOR: All the same, I'm going to ask you a regular pot-hunter's question now. What is the biggest fish ever caught at Stockbridge, as far as you know?

Plate IX

PISCATOR: 11 pounds 12 ounces. . . . Caught on a piece of meat! So your pot-hunting, as you call it, has been properly rewarded! That was in 1898, and in 1897, the Diamond Jubilee year, there was another of 10 pounds . . . caught on bread. But the best two on the fly are 6 pounds 9 ounces on a dry sedge, and 6 pounds 8 ounces on a wet fly.

VENATOR: Thank you. My greed for big fish is temporarily sated. And I perceive on these shelves a good antidote for even a 12-pounder caught on meat. . . . There is verily a harvest of quietude in these rows of old brown books. May I see some of them?

PISCATOR: Certainly; they are all on fishing. Here is a second edition of Dame Juliana, 1496. And here's another, a sixteenth-century quarto. She must have been a curious old lady, mustn't she, with her *Treatyse of Fysshynge with an Angle*?

VENATOR: I expect she would be astonished if she knew what controversies have raged about her—what arguments on the question of her name, and her identity, and even her sex! For some say, do they not, that she was a man; and some that she never existed at all . . . like the people who insist that Homer's *Iliad* was not written by Homer, but by another man of the same name. . . .

PISCATOR: Yes; but it is pleasant to think of her as a Lady Prioress, writing her *Treatyse* amid tranquil cloisters. . . .

VENATOR: I have asked you what was your greatest adventure in the catching of Test trout; and now I would like to hear your greatest adventure in the collecting of fishing books.

PISCATOR: Pot-hunting again!

VENATOR: I know; it is a vice of mine, this sniffing out romance like a dog searching for a buried bone.

PISCATOR: Here's a small bone for you, then: the first book of any value which I bought. I got it, when I was very young, for six pounds. Here it is: *The True Art of Angling*, 1697. This is rarer than the first edition, 1696. Here is another of my earliest purchases, an old fifteenth-century French book, *Livret Nouveau auql sont conte*. . . . *XXVII Receptes novelles et approuvez de prendre poissons, Cannes et Oysseaux avec les mains, Moclats Filets Mozses,* etc. It was only when I had occasion to consult the British Museum authorities, years later, that I discovered that it was the only copy ever recorded!

VENATOR: Those five Waltons in the corner—are they early editions?

PISCATOR: Yes. They happen to be the first five editions in their original bindings. They all have the Reverend H. S. Cotton's book-plate, and were sold at his sale in 1838. That makes them rather interesting; but if you will look inside this one, another copy of the third edition, 1661, I think you will find something more interesting still—here, on the fly-leaf, "For my friend honest Will Iles," with his signature "Iz. Wa." That is Walton's own hand-writing.

VENATOR: May I have a look?

PISCATOR: Do. . . . You have fallen very quiet all of a sudden!

VENATOR: Yes.

PISCATOR: Have you anything else you wish to ask me? Are you planning some new diabolical question? Shall we return to Test trout and your pot-hunting–12-pounders, caught on meat?

VENATOR: No, I think not. I am sorry to have been so suddenly silent; but old Izaak Walton has rather taken my breath away. His own handwriting! It's amazing, isn't it? I know it's unreasonable that one should find the contemplation of it so thrilling; but one cannot help it, somehow. I think really it is the essential *rightness* of that inscription that delights one. *"For my friend honest Will Iles."* One feels that there, precisely, is the authentic Waltonian touch. That, and nothing else, is what that dear, gentle man *ought* to have written; and it is exciting to find that that is what he actually did write. . . . *"For my friend honest Will Iles."* Let us leave it at that.

. . . I think that Walton's kind old ghost must be very close, in this friendly room. . . . Thank you, Piscator, very much.

CHAPTER XIII

by
Harry Plunket Greene

THE SOUND OF IT

The very hills have tumbled down
And stoned the valleys in their fall.
Only the waters of the Ch'in and Wei
Roll green and changeless as in days gone by.

L. CRANMER-BYNG (*From the Chinese poet Po-Chui, A.D. 772-846*).

A FEW years ago I saw a screen reproduction of dry-fly fishing. It was mayfly time and, judging from the activity of the fisherman, every fish in the river was on the rise and every fish was the biggest fish in the river. He must have been a famous sprinter in his youth. He raced from bush to bush like a cowman dodging a bull. He threw himself headlong on his knees and began, apparently, to beat off a swarm of hornets; only desperation could have driven the rod at the pace. His arm worked like the rat-tat of a postman; the drying-casts were a blur. I waited for the inevitable collapse from exhaustion, when suddenly he leapt to his feet and I realised that he was into a fish. It must have been an alligator. Sir Peter Chalmers Mitchell once told me that when he was an undergraduate at Oxford he turned two small alligators into the Cherwell. This must have been one of them. My friend in the picture can never have been so near to death in his life. At every pull of the line he shot forward to the water's edge and toppled over, and, just as he was about to fall into the animal's jaws, recovered himself by a miracle in the nick of time. Despair seemed to lend his feet wings, for he ran backwards even faster than he ran forwards. Suddenly (I have a suspicion that two or three hours of the fight were cut out of the reel here) I saw a torpedo leap out

T

of the water into the landing-net, and they all collapsed together on the bank. The alligator was a fraud; he was a pound trout.

I felt a subtle poison stealing through my mind. My friend was, I knew, a brilliant fisherman and a master of economy. I began to feel a vague distrust of him. Perhaps he kept his flawless technique for company, and when he was alone in the secret places he went the pace to beat the record. I had visions of him packing trout one on top of the other and despatching hampers to Billingsgate in the dead of night, setting night-lines, bombing mill-pools, damming carriers, biting his nails till daylight brought him to the slaughter again: a smiling villain, trusted and admired, exposed at last by the camera. And then I realised that he was only moving with the times, and that he was a victim of "speeding up."

As I lay in bed that night I pictured to myself Schubert's little trout-stream emerging from the hands of that movie-man. It rushed, and raced, and rattled to the sea, it dashed its head against the banks, it hurled its flotsam into space; sinister, sucking, its eddies were whirlpools, its ripples cataracts; the water-rats scurried across its treacherous surfaces like speed-boats on a haunted lough; the swifts and sedge-warblers fled to cover from its spate; relentless as a pestilence, cruel as a stoat, it swept on, leaving death and ruin in its trail.

And how would Schubert's little Bächlein fare in the wireless station if the balance and control man did not know and love his Müllerlieder?

Was this the little musician that sang "Wohin?"* and rhymed its mill-wheel to its rhythm:

* Whither?

-ab zum Tha - le rau - - - schen so...... frisch und wun - der - hell

ETC.

Was this the little trout-stream that used to play with the miller's boy when he was small, that whispered to him when he went to sleep o' nights and chattered to him when he awoke o' morns, that ran, and danced, and drowsed and dozed with him, that brought him tip-toe to its fairies and coaxed its pixies to sing to him, that beckoned him to his first glimpse of the maid of the mill in the meadow below, that chuckled when they met, and laughed when they kissed and, when the end came, wept as it sang his broken heart to sleep; the little stream that danced along its way, singing the song which all the rivers sing–the age-old question, "Whither? Whither?"–as they run for ever downhill toward the sea?

This river knew nothing of mill-wheels and had forgotten its lovers. It looked neither to the right nor to the left. Its eye was on the tall chimneys down the valley. In the pools where the fairies had curtseyed the jettisoned saucepans heaved in the mud; where the pixies had sung the rusty scrap-iron clanked a dirge. Through one factory on to the next it thundered, gathering foulness on its way, iridescent with oil and tar and effluent, opaque, sullen, its sweet song jarred to a raucous roar in the monstrous amplifier, its memories and romances drowned in the muddy waters of materialism.

Perhaps the same good Providence who saved our folk-music from oblivion will send us another Cecil Sharp to record the music of our rivers before it is too late. Maybe science and enterprise will presently come together and give us the living picture of their story. Some conglomerate machine, tuned by the loving hand of a fly-fishing engineer, may wind upon its reel the sights and scents and sounds of chalk-stream and salmon-river, so that years hence, when our country life is a thing of the past, and the factories run from Tweed to Torridge and the pylons spider the moors and valleys, some great-great-grandson of ours, stirred by a vague atavistic impulse as he watches the screen, may feel the *chug-chug* of the salmon, or see the boil of the sea trout, or smell the wild mint and the water weeds, and hear the sedge-warblers and the reeds and the line and the reel singing the song of the fly-rod.

In front of his eyes, as the curtain goes up, is a field of buttercups. They are late this year, but thicker and more beautiful than ever. They stretch like a sheet of gold to the line of dark flags which hide the river. On the far side is a green down standing out against the blue sky. On its top there is a round clump of trees, and out of its near side time has quarried a scollop of snow-white chalk. Such blue, and green, and white and gold could only be in company in England. Far up on the left a glimpse of the river shows blue in the distance; the cattle stand knee-deep in its shallows. Over their heads the poplars sway gently in the south-west wind. A bunch of horses are feeding in the foreground, and on the right a couple of cart-colts look over a gate, and sneeze and whinny the time of day to them. On the left is a group of chestnuts with red and white cows standing in their shade; you can hear them munching, and blowing, and swishing their tails. The rabbits dollop out of the hedgerow and sit up in the sun. A couple of moorhens stroll unconcernedly in and out of the flags by the river, while overhead the swifts swoop along and across, and the swallows dip to the water and rise and dip again; and, crowing a fanfare to herald his arrival, a cock-pheasant stalks from the shadows across his royal carpet of golden buttercups and diamond dew.

And now a man walks into the picture. He has a rod in his hand and a net at his belt. He is smoking a pipe, and his clothes look older than himself. He strolls leisurely along; you can hear the *swish swash* of his waders in the dewy grass. The horses lift their heads and look affectionately at him as he passes them. They are hunters, turned out for the summer, and belong to the brotherhood of sport. They snuff "Tight line!" to him and nod their heads up and down towards the river where the swallows are dipping and rising.

He evidently understands, for he quickens his pace till he gets close to the water. He lays the rod on the ground and creeps up on hands and knees and looks over the top of the flags. He is back in double-quick time and starts pulling out his line. But he is not half so excited as the reel. It chuckles, and growls and barks, and tears round and round in circles like a terrier starting out with the children. The cast is up now and the little winged fly also (hackles are no use to the camera-man); and then, with the rod held well out of sight, he crawls back to the bank and, kneeling on one knee, peers through the tops of the flags up stream.

Down the middle of the river on his right is a long bank of weeds, tremulous in the current and sparkling in the sun. On the left the water is deep and smooth. The bank is higher at this spot, and the current hugs it as it flows. It is dark here, with knife-edged shafts of light across the water where the sun cuts through the flags, and on the velvety surface the little duns come drifting down like fairy boats. As he watches, something stirs in the bay above the little weed-patch on the left, the water bulges up stream, and in the middle of one of the shafts of sunlight a big nose appears, and *left! right!* two of the fairy boats are gone—a big trout is on the feed!

[132]

Plate No. 3

Now the rod is at work, over the left shoulder, out of sight, slow, deliberate, finding the length. Is there anything more subtle than its rhythm, anything to compare in grace with the swan-neck curves of the line as it swings like a trapeze from high up in the dome, carrying the little gymnast on its handlebar ever nearer death or glory?

All round you, as you watch, are the river sounds–the rustle of the flags, the *umbuzz* of the bumble-bee disputing your title to the air, the sedge-warbler "calling your bluff," the pulsing of the pancake weeds, the *souping* of the feeding trout at the bend above, the cock-pheasant in the meadow on your left, the scutter of the moorhens down below you, and the laughter of the ripples as they dance along beside you in the sunlight. You hear them without knowing it, for something else has got you in its grip–there, far up under the bank, the little "iron-blue" has dropped among the fairy boats and is sailing down the eddies to the bay above the weed-patch on your left.

As he crosses the bar of sunlight something bulges the water below him, a big nose comes up, and a big mouth opens and with extreme deliberation sucks him out of sight.

On the instant the brothers leap to life.

"Who . . . oy! Tally-ho!" holloas the reel.

"Forrardy! forrardy!" cheers the rod.

"Yonder he goes!" shouts the line.

"'Loo at 'm!" cries the cast.

"Worry 'm and tear 'm!" mutters the iron-blue.

"Wake me when you want me," yawns the net.

Up stream he races in one long rush till the line sags upon the water in a curve and you feel sure that all is lost. But here he comes back again, faster than the reel can tackle him; the slack is in a jumble at your feet, but you have got the feel of him again. Up again and down again, fighting every inch of the way and edging always towards the weeds. Now he is back in his old home in the little bay, shaking his head and switching his tail. It is not as burglar-proof as it used to be; he will bolt into the big weed-patch on the right; once he gets his nose in there he will rub off the little blue bulldog. But those weeds are not nearly so hospitable as when he visits them on shrimping expeditions. You can see them heave and bulge, and a great tail come out and flail the air; something has made him an unwelcome guest–there is a little blue thing sticking in his nose, and it doesn't like weeds. Very well, he will race off down stream so fast that it won't be able to follow him. Down past you he rushes, hugging the bank; you can hear the thrum of his scurry under your feet; but the little blue bulldog is still there. Back he comes, turning, twisting, tugging, yielding slowly to the inexorable pressure of the rod. And then suddenly he catches sight of you! (Was it he or the reel who screeched?) He dashes past you in one headlong rush up stream, leaps into the air, sun-fishing like a bucking bronco, trying with head or tail to snap the cast, falls back on the water with a crack like a pistol-shot and, in the half-second of time before you can tighten-up on him again, plunges head-on into the very depths of the big weed-bed at the bend.

He is so far in, and so deep down, that you would not know he was there only for the line showing out of the water; the cast is out of sight. He is impervious to threats or blandishments. It is no use telling him you will knock his head off if he doesn't come out and fight, or assuring him that the new lot of iron-blues are much fatter than the old ones. He doesn't care as much about iron-blues as he used, and he is very comfortable lying "doggo" in the cool deep weeds, and if you have no objection he will now take a nap.

But the fisherman has something to say to this. He sticks the spike of his rod into the ground, and takes the line in his hand and pulls on it very gently. (Now, little gymnast, on your 4x handlebar, show your mettle!) Nothing happens for a moment. Then there is a commotion in the weeds. He seizes the rod and winds in the line, the reel shouting, "He's on! He's on!" as he gathers it in. The cast is showing now and heading towards the bank. Then a tail appears and then a head, and then a big fat side spotted red and silver in the sunlight, and slowly, very, very slowly, unaware, the big chalk-stream 3-pounder floats gently down on top of the water into the sleepy landing-net.

He is but the first of several on that June morning, though the brothers cannot always pull it off, and once the handlebar breaks and the little gymnast pays for it with his life. One of them was quite orthodox in his ways; another bored clean through a weed-bed and fought his battle out on the other side; another developed hydrophobia and spent his time imitating the letter S in the air; another never showed up till the end, but swam up and down in the deep places with the line cutting the water like a knife, and he was the best of the lot; and another who could not understand what all the fuss was about, and with an "Anything to oblige!" walked quietly into jail. And then the fun in the shallows where it is, "Pull devil, pull baker!" and anybody's game, and the little waves shout for joy and slap his waders as they dash past—so different from those sinister shallows above the black swirling pool in the Scottish salmon-river which hiss at you between their teeth: "One slip and you're lost!"

And then through buttercup-fields and water-meadows, with the dog-roses above and the blue water forget-me-nots below, past the early golden mimulus, bunches of glory in the sunshine, to luncheon at the tree below the old water-mill where the keeper lives. Crusoe, the cocker-spaniel, and Jack the Labrador, are fast asleep, with their heads in his lap. They had come rushing out, yelling with delight and thrown themselves all over him. Crusoe is all right; he leans up against you and looks up at you with eyes that are wells of pathetic appeals for sympathy. But Jack is a nuisance; he puts his paw in your face when he wants to attract your attention; also when you are into a fish he rushes up and down the bank singing at the top of his voice and dives on top of it as you bring it to shore. Jack is snoring now and Crusoe hunts in dreams, and their friend is gradually dropping off too. His pipe is sagging in the corner of his mouth. He blinks sleepily for a moment and chuckles to himself—a water-rat has just shouted " πομφολυγο-πάφλασμα " with a wicked twinkle in his eye and looked quickly the other way; nothing will ever persuade him that we do not eat frogs in England. The baby moorhen is under the same impression. She squeaks "Kerblink–kerblunk!" and dives for her life, while her mother calls to her out of the dark reed-bed and tells her not to be a fool. It is all no use. It is two o'clock on a hot June day; the cart-horses are bunched under the big beech tree close by; they stamp, and swish at the flies with their tails and doze in the shade; far up behind him the mill-wheel drones "Sumph, sumph"; the pigeons croon their bubbling coos to him from the roof; in his nostrils is the blessed smell of dog, and horse, and stable, and cottage-garden flowers; the poplars on the bank whisper "Hush! hush!"; the lime tree above his head hums with bees; the air is drowsy with "the live murmurs of a summer's day"—man, dog, reel, rod, line are all asleep, and the picture is done.

This is a fantasy. But the orbit of "our philosophy" widens from day to day. A few years ago, comparatively, the B.B.C. announcer would have been burned at the stake; and there are places still in these islands where Reason's writ does not run.

I have spent some of the most romantic times of my life in just such a spot —on a lough 60 miles from a station, in the middle of a moor so boggy that a pony cannot travel it, so remote that we, and the stags, and the eagles, and the peregrines, and a shepherd have it to ourselves. At Blagdon on a calm night you can hear the "plop" of a trout a mile away or talk to your friend across the lake without raising your voice. Up there it is a lone curlew or the bleat of a lamb far up on the mountain; but even on the stillest night the sea curls along the edges of the sandy bay with a roar like rolling thunder.

I once saw two stoats there play the time-honoured game of hide-and-seek exactly as we play it. I do not know where they came from or how they got there; they just appeared at my feet. They had never heard of guns or jazz or other lethal weapons, and either looked upon me as a benevolent feature of the landscape or wanted me to see the ripping game they had just invented. She took him up to a big stone, and told him to be a good boy and lie down behind it and count fifty, and off she raced and hid. When the time was up he jumped to his feet and scurried about until he found her, and they danced, and leapt over one another, and sparred and laughed till they cried. They did this again and again; and then she played him a trick. She put him behind an extra big stone and told him to count a hundred this time, and away she went at top speed right round the corner of the hill. He started out full of fun, springing into the air to see behind as many stones as possible; and then he began to run belly to earth, and then he began quartering the ground, getting faster and faster, till at last, screaming from sheer terror that he had lost her, he fled in panic clean out of sight. He found her, no doubt, in the end, and gave her a bit of his mind, but, poor little chap! he must have had a bad time.

The thing that impressed itself most upon me at the time was the velvet-pawed silence in which the greater part of the drama was played! They never made a sound and might have come straight out of one of Queen Mab's nature-films.

I was on the lough one sunny morning, nominally fishing for sea trout, and whistling for a breeze. It was a flat calm and perfectly hopeless. The little "brownies" were a nuisance, and I was tired of putting them back. I was pulling impatiently at one of these and using very bad language when suddenly I heard the reel say under its breath:

"Steady! Look out! Jungle-cock is trying to get a message through!"

I sat up and took a firm grip of the rod. The "brownie" swam slowly up to the boat and examined it from every side. He spent five minutes going round and round and underneath us, while we silently manœuvred out of his way. Suddenly there was a yell from the reel and out went 40 yards of line, and up into the air went a 10-pound salmon. That was my lucky day. It had gradually been growing darker as the fight progressed, and we had hardly got him on board when there came a clap of thunder and a roar and a hiss behind us, and we were in the middle of a squall, with the boat tossing about like a cork, and hanging on to a 5-pound sea trout into the bargain!

There is a haunted lough high up in those mountains, in among the corries where the stags are. It lies at the foot of an Etna-shaped peak on which the ravens live. It is as round as a saucer and so deep-set that it is generally dead-still. But one of our party was once caught there in a storm. He said that things suddenly went mad around him. Something seized his line and flogged him with it. No matter in what direction he tried to cast, it wound it round him in wisps and slashed the flies across his face. The air was full of voices. He was standing far out in the water, and they hissed him and cursed him and buffeted him to the shore, and when he got there he ran for his life.

That was his story. But who would dare, or care, to say that there are no fairies left? I came across a little stream some time ago in Rutland which did not belong to this world. It was a tiny Test which had escaped from fairy-land and was pretending to be a carrier. It ran through midget flags, and dwarf pollards, and wee tufts of blue forget-me-nots, and it hardly made a sound. I was trying to drop a fly into one of its diminutive pools, when I thought I heard a small frightened voice cry out and I saw something stir in the forget-me-nots, and I stopped.

There is another lake fuller far of fairies than the Rutland stream, and more remote than our mountain tarn. It is Moira O'Neill's famous "Fairy Lough," which the master-hand of Stanford has helped to immortalise in music.

Both the famous poem and the music are classics by now. I doubt if there is another pianoforte song in existence which contains so much imagery and musical illustration in a short space. I should like to show how it strikes the singer who looks at it from within, though at the end of it the reader may wonder what the singer has to do with it. It is not widely sung because the average singer, alas! does not realise that his only place in music is to deliver a message. The analysis is my own, and made without consultation with the composer, and does not profess to be anything but an imaginative picture inspired by the music.

THE FAIRY LOUGH*

Loughareema, Loughareema
   Lies so high among the heather;
A little lough, a dark lough,
   The wather's black an' deep.
Ould herons go a-fishin' there,
   An' sea-gulls all together
Float roun' the one green island
   On the fairy lough asleep.

Loughareema, Loughareema!
   When the sun goes down at seven,
When the hills are dark an' *airy*,
   'Tis a curlew whistles sweet!
Then somethin' rustles all the reeds
   That stand so thick an' even;
A little wave runs up the shore
   An' flees, as if on feet.

Loughareema, Loughareema!
   Stars come out, an' stars are hidin';
The wather whispers on the stones,
   The flittherin' moths are free.
One'st before the mornin' light
   The Horsemen will come ridin'
Roun' an' roun' the fairy lough,
   An' no one there to see.
                MOIRA O'NEILL.

---

* Messrs. William Blackwood and Sons and Messrs. Boosey and Co. have kindly given permission for the inclusion of the poem and of the musical extracts.

The "Fairy Lough" is a *berceuse.* It is rocked upon the little waves which carry the sleeping sea-gulls round and round the little green island for ever and ever.

An' sea-gulls all............ to - ge - - ther Float roun' the one green is - land

On the fair - y lough a - sleep.............................

Some of the waves are longer and deeper. When you first see the little black lake it seems to be breathing softly, almost imperceptibly.

But when they reach the shore they get very small, and run up the strand and back again and laugh under their breath.

e - - ven; A lit - tle wave runs up the shore An' flees,

And as you watch them you hear the curlew calling in the sky high up above the dark hills.

When the hills are dark...... an' *air* - - *y*, 'Tis a curlew whis-tles sweet !

And down below you hear the water whisper o'er the stones at your feet, and the moths flitter round your head; and as the first light comes up in the east you hear the Horsemen gallop up to tell them the day is at hand, and ride off into the distance.

The wa - ther whis-pers on the stones,.................. The flit-ther-in' moths are

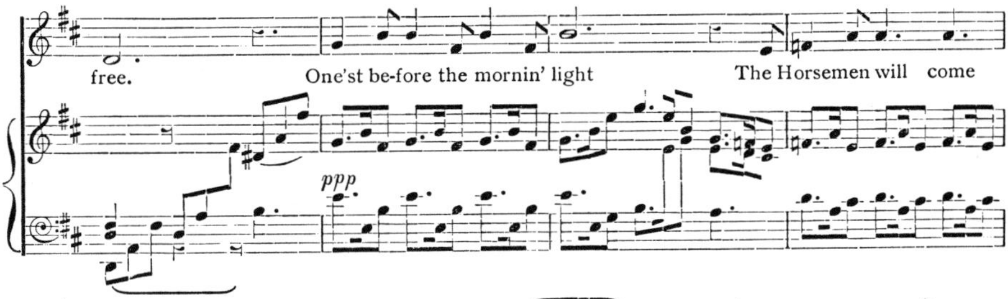

free. One'st be-fore the mornin' light The Horsemen will come

ri - - din' Roun' an' roun' the fair - - - - y lough,......................

An' no one there........... to
see.

Più lento.

Lough - - - a - reem - - - - - - - a! Lough - - - a -

reem - - - - - - - - a!

Three crowded minutes of imagination without a jostle anywhere! Here the sea-gulls float round the little green island for ever and ever asleep. Here, in the music, you can see the little waves run up the shore "an' flee as if on feet," and hear the "Coo-ee! Coo-ee!" of the curlews high up in the dark. The little lake "lies so high among the heather" that there is "no one there to see." Here the "Silver Swan" need never "lean her breast against the reedy shore, and sing her first and last and sing no more," for she need never die.

There are some of us who have never lost our fairies and who love the quiet places. We, of this generation, are the connecting link between the old days and the new, the bridge across the greatest chasm that has ever split the lives of men. Perhaps in a million years we may be gone and the trees will possess the earth, and their roots, as they grope down, may come across the fossilised remains of human civilisation; or maybe in a million years the machine may have worked out its salvation and earned an immortal soul. But some of us, if ever we win a place in the Elysian fields, will pray it may be in a quiet spot where we can smell the fallow and the sweating horses, and hear the swath of the scythe in the orchard, and go to bed by candlelight; or on some bank within sound of running water, where we can lie in the wild mint and watch the rising trout, and listen to the drumming snipe and the voice of the river singing the song which all the rivers sing—the age-old question, "Whither? Whither?"—as they run for ever downhill toward the sea.

CHAPTER XIV

by
Sir Charles Holmes

THE COLOUR OF IT

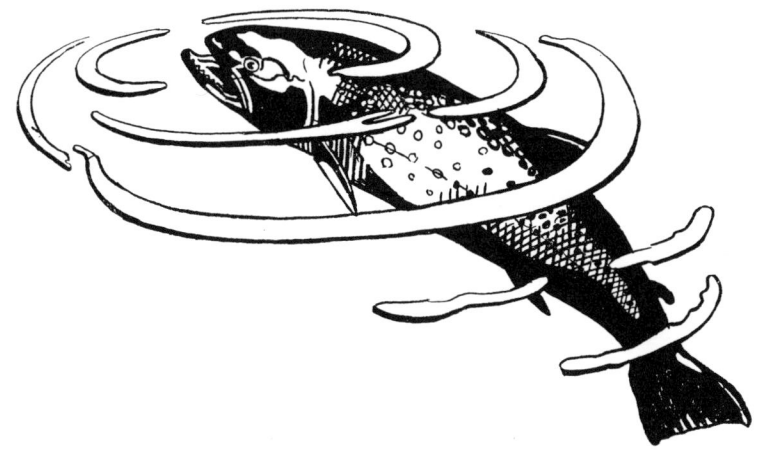

I HAVE a friend, and a proper fisherman, too, for whom the paraphernalia of angling, the glitter of a rod, the clean mechanic beauties of a reel, and above all the pageant of well-stored fly-boxes, form no small part of his pleasure in the craft. He spends the dark winter months poring in fascinated speculation over the sparkles of light, the spangles and flashes of colour, which some new pattern of minnow or tinselled fly exhibits when turned in his fingers under a lamp. Another friend, hardly less skilful, talks all the while of the birds he has watched by the waterside, of the flowers he has noticed, and of the scenery which, in his leisure moments, he sketches quite prettily. These pleasures are denied to me. Never a botanist, an ornithologist, nor an entomologist, I become on the river bank the dullest of fellows. If my rod glitters, the glitter gives me anything but pleasure. Were I not fundamentally an idler or a coward, I should cover the thing with a coat of good flake white. Indeed, in the north, where one has perforce to be much on the skyline, I should, but for the aforesaid defects of character, procure me white overalls and stalk my fish invisible. As for gaudy flies, the humble trout of my acquaintance will have none of them, and if I do happen to keep one or two small salmon flies in reserve, it is not for the charm of their bright feathers.

"The colour of it" surely begins with the water itself, that ever-changing medium through which we look down into another world—the world that is our happy hunting ground. Therein our fancy once attracted may wander at will from boyhood to old age, with no loss of interest, no tedium born of jaded experience, for even the most familiar water never remains quite the same. Floods and drought may not sensibly change its course, but more obscure forces are always at work to influence the tastes and behaviour of its inhabitants. You may have fished a river for forty years, but when the new season opens, can you be sure that it will be just like its predecessors? Can you estimate the alterations in the zoological balance, in the supply of food, the location of feeding grounds, the increase or decrease in hostile forces that the last six months have brought about? No doubt there are waters far from the reach of common mortals where the balance from year to year remains fairly stable; where there are neither men nor mills, nor motor cars and motor roads to befoul the water, nor predatory fish and birds and visitors with nets or dynamite to take unfair toll of its inmates. We may hear or read of such places, but few of us find them or have the chance of fishing in them. We must hold ourselves fortunate if fate has permitted us to try our luck once or twice on such Elysian waters, and allots us for regular use one or two modest stretches which still, in spite of ever-encroaching civilisation, do contain a few fish.

Possibly it is the sense of these vicissitudes, of our struggle with the inexorable destiny which year by year curtails our sport, that makes the sport so precious. Were all waters clean and well stocked, might not our interest in them diminish as our experience increases? Might we not find our success monotonous? It is uncertainty, not always glorious, that makes the game worth playing, and that keeps the eyes alert. Even the distant flash of water seen for a moment from a car or passing train gives a fillip to the attention, while the nearer view of any river, lake, or pond at once prompts mental speculation: "Where and how should I start fishing *that?*" "Are the fish many and small, or are they few and large?" "There is room in the corner under that bush for a fish of a pound or more." "How would one manage if one had leave to fish only from that farther bank with all those trees and bushes overhanging the water?" "With all that heavy weed, it's the dry fly or nothing." So the light and colour of pools that we never have fished, and never can hope to fish, become part of our lives, and may remain with us in memory when many far more positive and tangible happenings are altogether forgotten.

There is a point in the history of the oldest families where genealogy breaks down, and we come to mythology or to an honest confession of ignorance. But if by some freak of science, some superhuman antiquarianism, we could trace back our pedigree beyond the period of history, I suspect that every born angler, every man with the instinct for the water-side, would find that his enthusiasm came from some primitive ancestor who followed the humble fisherman's craft. Inborn it must be. Long before I had ever heard or read of angling, while I was still a tiny toddler in a frock, I found a sudden fairyland. At the foot of the vicarage field, under an arch of greenery, ran Water Lane, with a clear brown trickle down the middle of it which childish imagination enlarged to the dimensions of a river, flowing from the unknown to the unknown, every turn of it charged with infinite, inexpressible possibilities.

These possibilities soon took a more definite shape. Less than two miles off lay the Bude Canal. In the basin a coasting schooner was lazily unloading coal, and from the deck protruded a yellow fishing-rod, with a painted cork float below. Here was a mystery. "What strange things lived in that still, coal-black water?" "Fish?" "Then may *we* fish?" was the instant demand of two mites of five and three. In due course a resourceful nurse provided long pea-sticks, black thread, bent pins, and bread. I remember even then regarding the tackle with a distrustful eye; it somehow seemed inadequate. If a fish was large enough to swallow the generous cubes of bread (and such deep black water might hold any sort of monster) that stick and that thread would surely break? So when the infantile experiment was made, and failed to attract the dace and eels which (as later knowledge proved) managed to live in that unpromising fluid, there was no disappointment. On the contrary, there was perhaps a little satisfaction at seeming to be right, when the all-wise and much-enduring provider of necessities was wrong.

Years passed before black water was discovered again, in the tarns among the Coniston fells, but at once the blackness exercised its former fascination. Now the surroundings perhaps had something to do with it. The circle of dark summits round Levers Water in cloudy weather or at twilight took on a sinister look, and the deep water under them, though we caught nothing in it, seemed a gulf in which some primæval monster might still survive. One gloomy evening, indeed, the menace above and below became so acute that we fled from it in terror down the hillside. Shortly before, we had had evidence of what formidable beasts more innocent-looking waters might conceal. A chain of Lancashire mill-ponds contained an abundance of carp. To confound a friendly but sceptical butler we had set out to make a record catch, and in the process of doing so happened to take a ¼-pound roach. Roach were not in the day's programme, so the fish was returned. He wobbled somewhat feebly near the surface towards my float some three yards out. There was a gleam in the brown water, and an eel all green and silver and some 5 feet long serpentined to the top, took the roach by the middle as a trout might take a fly, and returned to the depths–a portentous apparition which haunts the memory still.

It was long ere the spell of darkness was broken. If a stream contained a big black pool, if the shore of any lake sloped steeply down to unfathomable gloom, that seemed the place to fish for a monster. The memory of the great eel, and legends of the giant *Salmo ferox*–for old books on fishing can corrupt the young no less thoroughly than new books on æsthetics–still haunted the imagination in the face of repeated failure. Slowly, very slowly, the conviction grew that large fish, though they might rest in these mysterious deeps, were wont to feed, and perhaps be hooked, in the less romantic shallows.

So much, then, for black water. And has anyone a good word for the black trout that come out of it? My memories are of things soft and white and flabby, often mere bags of bones–trout by species only. The trout proper, the trout that is good to look upon and to eat, comes from waters that in their deeps are golden brown, or greenish grey; and if this last has just a hint of white chalk in it the fish will be none the worse. In some such waters their delicate pink and silver is muted with a soft iridescence, as if, like Roman ladies, they were accustomed to bathe in cream.

Of these colours the browns are the most varied. At the bottom of the scale lie the dark porter-coloured waters that come from the peat. Old books often commend this colour to the fisherman. In my experience it is almost wholly baneful. Where it is a normal condition the fish are black and ill-nourished. Where, as in the Eden, it is exceptional, its appearance invariably spells disaster. The normal flood colour of the river is a turbid neutral brown full of reddish sand from the Permian rock. But one large tributary on Stainmoor runs through a peat bed, and in spate carries down masses of the dark soil, charged apparently with some acid matter which instantly puts the fish off their feed. The casual visitor will then find himself with a starving creel in the midst of conditions which seem ideal. Since these lines were first penned, a cloudburst on the moor has discharged this peat into the river in such quantities that the fish for a dozen miles or more, numbering many thousands, have been practically exterminated. One of my informants himself took out 140 gasping fish with a landing-net and placed them in fresh water to try and save them. So potent was the poison that on the next morning only 19 were still alive.

What, then, of sherry colour, golden-brown sherry? It can certainly look adorable whether in a wine glass or in a river. There in sunlight it will transmute every common pebble into a precious stone. A lapidary's window is not more gorgeous, especially when long trailers of weed, like serpents of green and gold, move here and there above the carpet of jewels. In the smaller upland streams this added beauty is no hindrance to the angler; indeed, it helps to make his person and his tackle less conspicuous. But in the main river the colour charms only to disappoint: it is too often the resplendent herald of next-to-nothing. During the full flood and the hours in which the stream has been running down, the fish have glutted themselves. By the time the golden-sherry stage has been reached they are slowly digesting their dinner, and will not be ready for another meal till the water has cleared still further. In lakes I have noticed that the colour is generally associated with masses of weed, plenty of fish food, and trout of more or less predatory habit who like the fly to be rather large and in lively motion.

The best of all browns in our local experience is the one that looks the least promising. After a flood, when the water still seems far too thick for the fly to be visible, a rise will often begin in the sluggish pools, if the weather be mild and windless. The fish, too, are really feeding in the chocolate or clay-coloured mixture, and not merely playing with the fly. Long ago I remember a rise of this kind in that capricious stream the Yore. A glorious evening sun had turned the turbid, oily surface to burnished gold, and for a full hour the dainty, difficult fish rose all round me. For several dry and cloudless weeks they had been invisible while I flogged the shrunken waters in vain with the finest of casts and points. Now those casts and points proved that they were misbegotten or (more probably) overworked. Eight several times did they fail me, and each time one of my precious tiny Tups (the only fly the trout seemed to fancy) was taken from me. All the best fish in the river seemed to be on the feed at once, yet if any but the finest points were used the fly was disregarded. What should have been an evening of triumph was thus turned to disaster.

Later experiences on the Eden drove the same lesson home. It would be natural to suppose that when a rise begins in a turbid stream, so turbid that the angler himself is invisible 20 feet away, the moment has come for indulgence in the luxury of using 3x points—a luxury it would be in that country of trees and bushes and shoulder-high weeds and barbed-wire fences crowning the high bank. But the fish will have none of it. Through the sand and mud they can tell the difference at once: 3x inspires contemptuous neglect or positive terror; 4x brings many short rises and last moment repentances; 5x alone will usually pass muster. The flies favoured on these occasions are tiny black midges or spiders on ooo hooks, and are taken far more freely when floating than when damp or half sunk. In such conditions the trout seem to leave their accustomed quarters, and to move down backwards with the current, taking flies *en route*. Each rise is a foot or so below its predecessor, and where the bank is open enough to permit pursuit, it is possible to follow a fish down stream, and finally, perhaps, to hook him 40 or 50 yards below the place where he showed himself first. Where such pursuit is impossible a frenzied effort must be made to cover the fish before he drifts out of reach; not always quite so simple as it looks, since it is impossible to guess exactly what course he will take between one rise and the next. Many a fish thus passes through the danger zone without having been once fairly covered, for in the thick water the fly must drift right over him or he will fail to see it.

Below the surface, however, the obscurity must be more apparent than real. Not only do the fish show much more suspicion of any half-sunk fly than of one which is fairly afloat, but their range of vision and sense of locality are much less impaired than one might think. About 18 yards away from the bank on which I was fishing there waved in mid stream the tip of a single rush, the sole survivor of a straggling clump which the floods of the previous spring had washed away. Owing to the oaks and beeches behind me I could not cast with safety for more than some 14 yards. My attention, therefore, was limited to such fish as came past within that narrow area. One of these, hooked well down stream, had to be handled gently owing to the drag of the current and a fallen bank which made it impossible to get down to level terms with him. Taking advantage of this momentary tenderness, the fish bolted out diagonally for some 5 or 6 yards straight towards that solitary rush, though it was above him and far out of his course. Could this downward dropping vagrant really be making for that remote little forlorn hope? It appeared incredible that he could either see it or know its exact whereabouts in that murky expanse. A momentary paralysis of wonder stayed my hand. In another moment all doubt was at an end. The trout was there, had taken firm hold, and refused to be cozened by relaxing pressure or to be moved by hand-lining. The fly was well and truly fixed into that rush, and had to be sacrificed; yet never was sacrifice made with a feeling so nearly akin to satisfaction. The fish had fairly won his freedom.

Indeed, as time passes, the old passion for a full creel sensibly weakens. Trout-fishing becomes more and more like a game of skill, played against an adversary who often exhibits so much resource and spirit that we are thrilled by scoring even a minor point against him, and may be genuinely grieved (unlike the walrus) when victory involves knocking our honourable opponent on the head. Now and then one may go so far as to return some solitary and sporting fish caught at the end of a blank day—especially if he happens to be just too small to redeem the credit of an empty basket, and to provide a respectable addition to the normal family breakfast. But this is not always possible. On the Bindweed, for example, the rising trout is a rarity. He seldom cares to leave his subaqueous Ritz-Carlton grill-room where, with a cold eye for the plebeian chub and a wary one for the pike, he stuffs himself at ease all the year round. But now and then in the spring the gauzy frills and flutterings of the too ephemeral mayfly tempt him upstairs to look at the pretty things. "Have at him!" must then be the angler's motto. Such a lapse may not recur for another twelvemonth. So from the first it is a battle à outrance with a doughty foeman, who happens incidentally to be the best eating in the world. A sea trout is not more pink, more firm, more delicately flavoured, nor, to complete the parallel, more disconcerting in his agility.

A few months ago the only visible fish was rising in a reach that was glassy and unruffled. Prudence advised the addition of a new 3x point to the cast, and from haste it is possible that the knot was but roughly trimmed. I have never conquered the boyish habit of biting off loose ends. By some miracle the first cast landed just as it should. The fish rose without suspicion, was firmly hooked, and in his surprise made a couple of jumps so quickly that the eye could only appreciate their complexity without following their course. In due time, however, he was drawn towards the net, a fish of just under 2 pounds, with a curious appendage trailing from his mouth. It was a loop in the cast some four inches across, and tied so tightly round the last knot that it could only be released by breakage. Such exceptional activity is a new feature on this river. Once upon a time its lordly trout had the water to themselves except for sundry things of no account, eels, crayfish, and vulgar, pushing families of chub. Then they could guzzle at ease like aldermen, and when hooked were apt to be fat and scant of breath. During the last three years, however, pike have made their way into this gastronomic Elysium, and haunt each roomy and comfortable pool. The chub suffer most. Hardly one in five appears to have survived the invasion. But the trout are clearly having no easy time. They have to be constantly on the alert, with muscles in perfect condition, if they are to escape the rush and the snap which is becoming too common an incident in the day's experience. The pleasures of the epicure, in fact (as Gibbon might put it), have to alternate with the activities of the gymnast. Whether gymnastics can ultimately save the trout remains to be seen. The pike, when they have finished off the chub, may develop under the spur of necessity a new turn of speed.

But I am wandering too far from my theme. The colours of the sky and the landscape, in theory at least, are among the chief attractions of our craft. But what can I say about them that is new, or has not been said much better by other fishermen, or recorded in drawings like those of the late Mr. E. E. Briggs, aglow with the light and colour of so many Scottish lochs and rivers? The brightness of April sunshine upon white walls, grey-green fields, and leafless woods; the pageant of blossom and tender, sprouting foliage in mid-May; the flash of a kingfisher at any time, are impressions which only a dullard could fail to register. But for myself I find that art and angling go ill together. When something wonderful in the sky or landscape does distract the eye from the water, the hand, shaken with much casting, refuses to do its office. The pencil strokes will stray this way and that; things will tumble into the wrong places. It is easier to draw in a motor-car or a railway train than by the river bank. Moreover, the effects of light and weather that force themselves upon the eye are usually just those that experience proves to be preludes to failure. A dull, damp day when a hueless sky hangs heavy over a leaden stream, and even the waterside flowers have their gaiety muted by the universal drabness, often yields the best basket. The artistic eye may delight in the glittering sunshine of a breezy day, or in the glowing hour that precedes the sunset when the woods flame upwards and downwards from the water's edge, but in our little corner of the world these pageants of light and colour seldom help to fill the creel. The light usually makes the angler show up as a portentous gesticulating giant, and invariably reveals the falsity of his lures.

Yet these moments have their magic, if only from contrast with other conditions. When I first sat me down by the Bindweed to think over "The Colour of It," the sky was heavy with cloud, the river a sheet of slightly greasy pewter, rasped by sudden wind-squalls. The spring was over. The bending willows had lost their freshness, the poplars their tones of gold. The meadow was grown nearly waist-high, yet the glaucous green of the rushes topped it by 2 feet or more. That was the colour of it, and of many another day in these declining times. It was not so always. There were halcyon days once, when meadow, grove, and stream did seem apparelled in a light which, if not quite celestial, was at least more glorious and exhilarating than any which shines upon me today. The air was then more fresh, the world more full of fruit and flowers and fragrance. If there were showers they were always followed by bursts of sunshine; indeed, I can only recall one angling morning when I got relentlessly soaked to the skin, and that was followed by a blazing afternoon. Memory is evidently like the old tag on the sundial, *Horas non numero nisi serenas.*

Even the dismal day of which I speak had its thrills. A minor one came first, when a fish which I had marked three weeks before, and sought from both banks and every accessible standpoint, suddenly took my fly where neither he nor it should have been, and then, leaving the weeds and willow branches between which he had wandered, jumped up madly into an open pool where he was duly netted. A sorry business it was, reflecting no credit upon either of us. Still, on such a dripping hopeless day a fish was a fish. Ten minutes later the west began to lighten, revealing bright cloud bars with storm-tossed cumulus behind them. Next came the sun; no misty orb, but a fierce searchlight that turned the meadows to gold and the willows to emerald. For a while the river showed as a sheet of lustrous purple-black amid all this glowing splendour, which, as the blue spread to the zenith, changed to silver and azure. Evening was coming on, yet not one rise dimpled the level surface. The reason was soon apparent. As I turned for a last look at the water before driving away the light grew dim. A great pyramid of darkness was rising in front of the sun, and half an hour later the whole countryside disappeared behind grey curtains of rain. That, in this season of perpetual storm, has too frequently been "The Colour of It."

CHAPTER XV

by

Eric Parker

THE POETRY OF IT

AND of what form or use of the fly-rod should the poetry deal first, and what should be the scene of the fishing? Should it be the banks of the Aberdeenshire Dee in February, with the snow pencilled blue in shadow, and the golden plover crying on the hill? Or Tweed, deep and brown under an autumn wood, and sunset behind Eildon? Or Test, with the sky between its cresses, and sedge-warblers in the willows, and the whir of landrail beyond the carriers? Or estuary waters, grey at dusk, and sea trout far from the boat, pulling the rod down to moonlight ripples? Or some Highland burn of August, dropping from pool to pool under heather and rowan, and little yellow trout flipping back into the peat water from the spume. . . .

Well, as to all that, of one point I am assured, that not all the poetry of fishing is intimately or definitely connected with rod or line, or with any particular river, or, indeed, with knowledge of fishing at all. For Shakespeare made one of the best of all angling poems when he wrote of the time

"When daffodils begin to peer,
With heigh! the doxy over the dale."

And Browning, when he wrote of the year at the spring, and Wordsworth when he began his twenty lines of March sun just with four words, "The cock is crowing," and Wordsworth again when he sees the rainbow–all these are in the heart of an angler when he walks by any river, and all of them must be for him in any book of poems of fishing, and none of them were written intentionally for him.

Perhaps that is natural. For it seems to be true, too, that when a poet sets out deliberately to write of what an angler does, and how he catches his fish, he fails in other directions. The eighteenth-century poets, Gay and Thomson, for instance, never knew the air that blows about a trout-stream. This is John Gay, in *Rural Sports*:

> "Far up the stream the twisted hair he throws,
> Which down the murm'ring current gently flows,
> When if or chance or hunger's powerful sway
> Directs the roving trout this fatal way,
> He greedily sucks in the twining bait,
> And tugs and nibbles the fallacious meat. . . ."

And this, of tying a fly:

> "To frame the little animal, provide
> All the gay hues that wait on female pride,
> Let nature guide thee; sometimes golden wire
> The shining bellies of the fly require;
> The peacock's plumes thy tackle must not fail,
> Nor the dear purchase of the sable's tail."

And here is James Thomson in *The Seasons*—a little better to begin with:

> "Just in the dubious point where with the pool
> Is mixed the trembling stream, or where it boils
> Around the stone, or from the hollowed bank
> Reverted plays in undulating flow,
> There throw, nice-judging, the delusive fly . . ."

but not so good to end with:

> "Till floating broad upon his breathless side,
> And to his fate abandoned, to the shore
> You gaily drag your unresisting prize."

In fact, this is not poetry but verse. Michael Drayton (but he was earlier, and nearer Shakespeare) wrote better of the life of the fisherman than either Gay or Thomson, and set him in his boat familiar with

> "Every pearl-pav'd ford and every blue-ey'd deep."

But even he made finer work of the forester than the fisher:

> "The dryads, hamadryads, the satyrs and the fauns
> Oft play at hide-and-seek before me on the lawns;
> The frisking fairies oft, when horned Cynthia shines,
> Before me as I walk dance wanton matachines. . . ."

Isn't that all in the moonlight? And as for the sunshine of fishing, which somehow is never set in the balanced iambics of Gay and Thomson, you must go back among these earlier writers to the *Compleat Angler* itself, and then look for spring and summer, not among poetry dealing with fishing first, but in poems quoted, not made, by Walton. In this of Sir Henry Wotton's, written "when he was beyond seventy years of age . . . of a part of the present pleasure that possessed him":

> "This day Dame Nature seem'd in love;
> The lusty sap began to move;
> Fresh juice did stir th' embracing vines,
> And birds had drawn their valentines.
> The jealous trout, that low did lie,
> Rose at a well-dissembled fly. . . ."

That was a day in April, perhaps? The *Compleat Angler* itself begins with Piscator setting off up Tottenham Hill on a pleasant fresh morning in May. And to May belongs the milkmaid's song, with its simple quatrains, "much better," Piscator thinks, "than the strong lines that are now in fashion in this critical age":

> "A belt of straw and ivy buds,
> With coral clasps and amber studs;
> And if these pleasures may thee move,
> Come live with me, and be my love."

That is the May sunshine that lies about the *Compleat Angler,* and it is that, rather than verse directly to do with rods and tackle, that has gone to the heart of every reader since Lamb, writing to Robert Lloyd of his spirit *"filled* with the scenes–the banks of rivers–the cowslip beds–the neat ale-houses–and hostesses and milkmaids, as far exceeding Virgil and Pope as the *Holy Living* is beyond Thomas à Kempis."

And to come next into that atmosphere you must travel through the seventeenth and eighteenth centuries–indeed a very long way beyond Pope–into the middle of the nineteenth, to find yourself in the spring again:

> "Is the cuckoo come? Is the cuckoo come?
> Seek ye its happy voice
> Bidding the hills rejoice,
> Greeting green summer and sweet May morn."

That is Thomas Tod Stoddart, author of *An Angler's Rambles* and *Angling Songs.* And if he does but mention "the lone angler towards the lake" in a single line in that poem, it still comes first to my mind among his songs, because the cuckoo is nearly all the spring for me, and because across the years, more clearly than in any other of his writings, you can hear the voice of the man himself.

[157]

Stoddart is the first modern poet who has set himself the task of writing poetry about angling and who has succeeded in bringing to the printed page the wind and the light of the river. He can be wholly simple, as in—

" The yellow fins o' Yarrow dale!
    I kenna whar they've gane tae;
Were ever troots in Border vale
    Sae comely or sae dainty?

"They had baith gowd and spanglit rings,
    Wi' walth o' pearl amang them;
An' for sweet luve o' the bonny things
    The heart was laith to wrang them."

And he can surprise with his choice of epithets, to bring into his book the gleam of a waterfall or the music of his beloved Tweed:

"I've angled far and angled wide,
On Fannich drear, by Luichart's side,
    Across dark Conan's current;
Have haunted Beauly's silver stream,
Where glimmering thro' the forest Dream
    Hangs its eternal torrent. . . .

"But dearer than all these to me
Is sylvan Tweed; each tower and tree
    That in its vale rejoices!
Dearer the streamlets one and all,
That blend with its Æolian brawl
    Their own enamouring voices!"

Stoddart collected his *Angling Songs* into a book in 1839. Nearly twenty years later Charles Kingsley, who had not yet published his *Chalkstream Studies*, was writing his delightful *Invitation* to Tom Hughes:

"Come away with me, Tom,
    Term and talk are done;
My poor lads are reaping,
    Busy every one.
Curates mind the parish,
    Sweepers mind the court;
We'll away to Snowdon
    For our ten days' sport;
Fish the August evening
    Till the eve is past,
Whoop like boys at pounders
    Fairly played and grassed.
When they cease to dimple,
    Lunge, and swerve, and leap,
Then up over Siabod,
    Choose our nest, and sleep."

Plate X

I daresay Kingsley wrote that in half an hour, but it has the breath of the mountain in it. And as for another piece of writing of his which has been called doggerel, I wish there were more such verse written, to carry their echo to other fishermen looking forward to a holiday:

"O blessed drums of Aldershot!
O blessed south-west train!
O blessed, blessed Speaker's clock,
All prophesying rain!"

Rather oddly, Kingsley wrote only two or three poems of trout-fishing, all haphazard stuff; he kept the best writing of his favourite sport for *Chalkstream Studies.* I wonder whether he ever met another clergyman-poet, who was making some of the best dialect poetry in the language about the same time, William Barnes. Like Stoddart, Barnes takes a fisherman with him through other poems besides those that have to do with fishing. First of all Barnes's poems that I read—and having read that one, I read through all that he wrote—was "The Woodlands":

"Oh, spread ageän your leaves an' flow'rs,
Lwonesome woodlands! zunny woodlands!
Here underneath the dewy show'rs,
O warm-aired spring-time, zunny woodlands!
As when in drong or open ground
Wi' happy bwoyish heart I vound
The twitt'rèn birds a buildèn round
Your high-boughed hedges, zunny woodlands!"

That took me back, for whatever reason, to the little Beane in Hertfordshire where in a schoolboy's holidays I was set in April to catch pike in a chalkstream, and listened to nightingales, driving home to dream of trout casts and flies of my own. But the woodlands belong, of course, to Dorset, and when Barnes writes of rivers it is of the Stour. And I think only once a fly-fisher walks by those winding banks, in "The Mead A-mow'd":

"When sheädes do vall into ev'ry hollow,
An' reach vrom trees half athirt the groun';
An banks an' walls be a-lookèn yollow,
That be a-turn'd to the zun gwaïn down;
Drough hay in cock, O,
We all do vlock, O,
Along our road vrom the meäd a-mow'd.

"An' when the visher do come, a-drowèn
His flutt'ren line over bleädy zedge,
Drough groun's wi' red thissle-heads a-blowèn,
An' watchèn o't by the water's edge;
Then he do love, O,
The best to rove, O,
Along his road drough the meäd a-mow'd."

And with Barnes, who was born in 1800 and lived to be eighty-six, we come to the moderns. And first among them to Andrew Lang, who, I have heard people say, was not as skilful a fisherman as he was a writer, and who has told us himself, in one of the most delightful pages ever given to a printer, that he is a duffer, but whose love for angling and for the Border rivers glows in every line he writes about them. In this, for instance, from *Ballades in Blue China*:

> "The ferox rins in rough Loch Awe,
>   A weary cry frae ony toun;
> The Spey, that loups o'er linn and fa',
>   They praise a' ither streams aboon;
>   They boast their braes o' bonny Doon:
> Gie *me* to hear the ringing reel
>   Where shilfas sing, and cushats croon
> By fair Tweedside, at Ashiesteel."

But he touches deepest, I think, in "Twilight on Tweed," in *Grass of Parnassus* :—

> "Three crests against the saffron sky,
>   Beyond the purple plain,
> The kind remembered melody
>   Of Tweed once more again.
>
> "Wan water from the Border hills,
>   Dear voice from the old years,
> Thy distant music lulls and stills
>   And moves to quiet tears. . . .
>
> "A mist of memory broods and floats,
>   The Border waters flow,
> The air is full of ballad notes
>   Borne out of long ago.
>
> "Old songs that sung themselves to me,
>   Sweet through a boy's day-dream,
> While trout below the blossom'd tree
>   Plashed in the golden stream."

But it was as a fisherman, too, and not only as a poet, that the author of *Grass of Parnassus* was known to his friends. When Stevenson writes to

> " Dear Andrew, with the brindled hair,"

it is to one gifted with an "equal craft of hand" with pen and fly-rod:

> "I count you happy starred; for God,
> When he with ink-pot and with rod
> Endowed you, bade your fortune lead
> For ever by the crooks of Tweed,
> For ever by the woods of song
> And lands that to the Muse belong;

> Or if in peopled streets, or in
> The abhorred pedantic Sanhedrin,
> It should be yours to wander, still
> Airs of the morn, airs of the hill,
> The plovery Forest and the seas
> That break about the Hebrides,
> Should follow over field and plain
> And find you at the window pane;
> And you again see hill and peel,
> And the bright springs gush at your heel."

When *Grass of Parnassus* was published, Mr. Alfred Cochrane was playing cricket for Oxford; and I do not doubt that he read it between the innings, so to speak. For he follows next to Andrew Lang to Parnassus slopes, and finds the same flowers there. His poem "The Fishermen," with its current moving calm or quickened with chalk-stream or salmon-pool, demands for his *Collected Verses* a place on every fly-fisher's bookshelf:

> "The quiet pastime of their choice
>   On Beauly rocks, in Derwent glades,
> Still seems to move to Walton's voice,
>   Singing of dace and dairymaids:
> His water meadows still are wet,
>   His brawling trout-streams leap and glance,
> And on their sunlit ripples yet
>   The flies of his disciples dance. . . .
>
> "Whether their lingering footsteps pass
>   Where Hampshire meadowlands are green,
> And where the chalk stream clear as glass
>   Goes by the pollard tops between;
> Where when the warbler folds his wings,
>   And the pale summer moon comes out,
> The scented breath of twilight brings
>   The sacred hour of moving trout—
>
> "Whether the river calls them forth,
>   That once a brown and modest burn
> Splashed down some hillside of the North
>   Through purple heather tufts and fern;
> That now flows on, a mighty tide,
>   From silent pool to chattering reach,
> Through whose dark depths the salmon glide
>   Beneath the rowan and the beech. . . ."

Mr. Cochrane's verses themselves are like well-tied flies—they allure with colour, neatness, glitter, and we must look at them side by side in their book. Another Oxford poet succeeds him, Mr. John Buchan. Mr. Buchan has written more than one poem of fishing, and his "Theocritus in Scots: The

Fishers" is a *tour de force* in translating the Doric of the Twenty-first Idyll into the vernacular of Lasswade colliers. Tam hooks a "maist enormous fish," which runs up stream "as wild as Job's Leviathan":

> "And syne he turned a dorty jaud,
>   Sulkin' far doun amang the stanes.
> I tapped the butt to stir his banes.
> He warsled here and plowtered there,
> But still I held him ticht and fair,
> The water rinnin' oxter-hie,
> The sweat aye drippin' in my e'e.
> Sae bit by bit I wysed him richt
> And broke his stieve and fashions micht
> 'Til sair fordone he cam to book
> And walloped in a shallow crook."

But if I am to choose one only of Mr. Buchan's poems for an anthology, it shall be "Fisher Jamie." In its humour, its *desiderium*, its reflected glow of lights on wood and stream, it surely stands alone. Fisher Jamie has been killed in the War, and now he is in a happier land, or ought to be. But Jamie knows no music but the song of the river, and instead of his "croun o' gowd" he will be thinking of "a kep o' dacent tweed" in which he can stick his casts. This is not his Heaven:

> "If Heaven is a' that man can dream
>   And a' that honest herts can wish,
> It maun provide some muirland stream,
>   For Jamie dreamed o' nocht but fish.
>
> "And weel I wot he'll up and speir
>   In his bit blate and canty way,
> Wi' kind Apostles standin' near
>   Whae in their time were fishers tae.
>
> "He'll offer back his gowden croun,
>   And in its place a rod he'll seek,
> And bashfu'-like his herp lay doun
>   And speir a leister and a cleek.
>
> "For Jims had aye a poachin' whim;
>   He'll süne grow tired wi' lawfu' flee
> Made frae the wings o' cherubim,
>   O' castin' ower the Crystal Sea. . . .
>
> "I picter him at gloamin' tide
>   Steekin' the backdoor o' his hame
> And hastin' to the waterside
>   To play again the auld, auld game;
>
> "And syne wi' saumon on his back,
>   Catch't clean against the Heavenly law,
> And Heavenly byliffs on his track,
>   Gaun linkin' doun some Heavenly shaw."

I think no other poet of angling could have written that. And as Mr. Buchan stands alone on the shelf as regards that particular poem, so there is one other poet who stands alone on certain banks of water: one who has written more verse of fishing than anyone else writing today, and verse of a texture all his own—Mr. Patrick Chalmers. I find it hard to choose from what he has written of trout-streams and of salmon-rivers. This, perhaps, of salmon:

"It's oh, but I'm dreaming
Of grey water streaming,
Great rivers that go gleaming
    Where brown the heather blows,
Ere May's southern graces
Rub out the last white traces
From high and mountain places
    Of stubborn, storm-packed snows!

"The chill wind that searches
The low-lying birches,
The old red grouse that perches
    And swaggers in the sun;
I'm fain for its blowing,
I'm restless for his crowing,
And it's I that would be going
    Where the spring salmon run!"

And this of sea trout. He writes of a Western isle:

"Grey it is, and very still
    In the August weather;
Grey the basking seals that flock
On their jaggèd lift of rock;
Starkly heaves a waste of hill
    Grey, untouched of heather!

"Grey streams show, by cliff and hag,
    Pools, and runs that riot,
There the great grey sea-trout rise
Splashing silver at your flies,
There the grey crow from the crag
    Croaks across the quiet!

"That's the place where I would be,
    Where the winds blow purely;
For I hear, by Fancy blest,
All the Fairies of the West
Sound their silver pipes for me—
    Horns of Elfland surely!"

But there is one poem in which Mr. Chalmers reaches a deeper chord, sends a fuller enchantment from the river of his thought, than any other writer of today. That is a poem in *A Peck of Maut*, "Below the Weir." I quote it in full:

> "Beyond the punt the swallows go
> Like blue-black arrows to and fro,
> Now stooping where the rushes grow,
>   Now flashing o'er a shallow;
> And overhead in blue and white
> High Spring and Summer hold delight;
> 'All right!' the blackcap calls, 'All right!'
>   His mate says from the sallow.
>
> "O dancing stream, O diamond day,
> O charm of lilac-time and May,
> O whispering meadows green and gay,
>   O fair things past believing!
> Could but the world stand still, stand still
> When over wood and stream and hill
> This morn's eternal miracle
>   The rosy Hours are weaving!
>
> "Eternal, for I like to think
> That mayflowers, crimson, white, and pink,
> When I am dust the boughs shall prink,
>   On days to live and die for;
> That sun and cloud, as now, shall veer,
> And streams run tumbling off the weir,
> Where still the mottled trout rolls clear
>   For other men to try for.
>
> "I like to think, when I shall go
> To this essential dust, that so
> I yet may share in flowers that blow,
>   And with such brave sights mingle,
> If tossed by summer breeze on high
> I'm carried where the cuckoos cry
> And dropped beside old Thames to lie
>   A sand-grain on a shingle.
>
> "Meanwhile the swallows flash and skim
> Like blue-black arrows notched and trim,
> And splendid kingcups lift a brim
>   Of gold to king or peasant,
> And 'neath a sky of blue and white
> High Spring with Summer weaves delight:
> 'All right!' the blackcap calls, 'All right!'
>   And life is very pleasant."

I knew that poem by heart the day when I first read it: I have thought it through many times since. For me it is all that the Thames, all that the English summer holds, sometimes almost all that there is of hope of other summers. It is an air from another world; I know no other poem that so lifts the heart of a fisherman.

CHAPTER XVI

by
John C. Moore

DE MINIMIS

"Forsan et haec olim meminisse juvabit."
Virgil.

I HAVE often wondered how water-diviners choose those little sticks which they hold so lightly between their fingers and which jump so violently (they say) when the hidden well is approached. Is one stick more powerful, more magical, than another? Do these men pluck any twig off any tree, or do they go prowling about the countryside, do they search high and low through the coppices or lurk in the hazel-brakes, balancing the small wands upon their fingers, testing them for resiliency, selecting one after they have cast a thousand away?

The purchase of a fly-rod (which is just as magical a weapon) is surely ridiculously simple by comparison. Granted the first necessity, that of possessing enough money (or being able to bluff your way into obtaining enough credit), it is an easy matter indeed. You walk into a pleasant shop where the cases of feathered witcheries in the window act as a deadly bait for anglers long before they come to their chief business of being a lure for fishes, and there a score of shining pieces of split cane are neatly arrayed for your choice. It is a brief affair to select one; each, as you take it in your hand, feels more beautifully alive, more delicately balanced, than the last. You flick them gently in turn, and perhaps you smash an electric-light shade, or poke another customer in the eye as he comes in through the door; but such mishaps are soon remedied by smooth words, and so anon you are out in the street again, carrying your precious bundle precariously through the crowds of hurrying Philistines.

You have achieved something more than the purchase of a piece of varnished bamboo, a contraption made of strips of cane hexagonally glued together and whipped with silk; your transaction has not been a mere prosaic item of business, as it would have been had you bought a pair of shoes, or a shirt, or a new hat. For in half an hour you have taken a ticket to Fairyland.

The bundle under your arm is a magic wand, no less. It will provide the motive and the impetus, as it were, which will send you, perhaps, tearing fifty miles in a day when the mayfly is up on some southern chalk-stream, or hundreds of miles north when one fine September you hear of a run of sea trout in a swift Scottish river. It is a rod as magical as Aaron's, which could conjure a snake from the bare rock. Flick it, and *hey presto!* you are out of the dirt and noise of London and beside a Cotswold brook on a May morning, with a repetitive chiff-chaff talking in a willow tree above your head and a cuckoo emphasising from afar the sweet sadness of the spring. Flick it again, and you are on the bank of a Welsh lake, where the savage beautiful mountains rise up all round you, an awesome company, with the fading bracken a-smoulder on their slaty slopes. Flick it a third time, and Devonshire with its red lanes and little green hills is yours; or Hampshire with its quiet woods and crystal rivers; or some wild northern isle, whose serried lochs open on "the foam of perilous seas"; or Westmorland with its great lakes and its deep black tarns up on the high fells.

All this will your fly-rod do for you—and more. Not only will it open up a new world, transporting you like a magic carpet in the Persian tales, but it will teach you, unless you are an unwilling pupil indeed, a new philosophy; not, perhaps, a complete theory of life, not a cosmic certainty, but at least a panacea for happiness—*the joy of little things*.

That is something which is rather difficult to define; when we were boys we all had it, for the world seemed new and exciting then, but when we grew up things lost their old fascination for us, became commonplace one by one, and we ourselves became very preoccupied with the major business of making money, or falling in and out of love, or with deep knowledge or abstruse philosophy. The little things were forgotten, or thrown into the limbo of friendly memories; we lost our eager delight in them, and perhaps we were none the better for it.

What are they, these trifles? Take a fragment from Rupert Brooke's catalogue of his loves:

> ". . . footprints in the dew;
> And oaks; and brown horse-chestnuts, glossy-new;
> And new-peeled sticks; and shining pools on grass . . ."

Were not these *your* old loves too? The strange inexplicable delight of whittling a brown twig into wet and glossy whiteness—and the game called 'obbly-'onkers, which you played with horse-chestnuts (how delightfully cold and damp and shiny they were when they first came out of their prickly shells!)–and the prints of unknown feet on short-cropped grass when it was grey with dew before the sunrise, footprints that seemed to vanish nowhither and to come nowhence?

Little things, no doubt, and not very significant; I question whether you would find the same delight in them now; but it would be a delight worth re-capturing all the same, if you are growing a little too serious, for these trifles have a way of giving a useful jolt sometimes to a mind which is running in a groove or is slightly out of balance. They give you back your sense of pro-portion, and they make you laugh again.

That shining split-cane fly-rod of yours, like the wand with which the Fairy Queen in a pantomime conjures forth her chorus, is an open sesame, as it were, to this world of little things. Flick it, take your ticket to Fairyland; and in half an hour you will have forgotten all your grave preoccupations, business, science, love, philosophy. Your rod has done more than transport you; it has changed you. Your sense of values is temporarily reversed; and it seems to you that it is tremendously important, more important than anything else in the world, that the river should be the right colour, the hatch of fly plentiful, the fish in the right mood. You become very concerned with the correct set of a tiny feather on a hook; you tie a small knot meticulously; you hear the "plop" of a rising fish up stream, and you go down on your hands and knees, Gravity crawling on his belly through a bed of stinging-nettles. All this is very good for you; you cannot creep *ventre à terre* in Oxford Street or Piccadilly.

As the day goes on, you lose your serious self still more thoroughly. In the intervals between fishing, flowers and birds begin to exercise their old fascina-tion over you. You notice with delight the patch of loosestrife–love's strife–blazing purple on the bank; it is like meeting unexpectedly with a well-loved friend whom you have not seen for many years. A starling perches 30 yards away from you, making a noise like someone sucking oranges, and you re-member another starling who made a similar sound long ago, and wonder wickedly whether you could hit this one with a catapult now; for that previous starling heard the flick and hiss which even Goliath once heard, and there was a sudden cessation of his noise, and a thud, and a flutter of feathers. That was thirty years ago, when you were adventurous and bloodthirsty and dirty-kneed; you would not send that pebble (that pebble as round as David's) so deadly straight now, at 30 yards' range. . . .

There are a good many things which you could then do, but which you would find far from easy nowadays. It is a blow to your self-respect, but it is good for your sense of proportion to realise it. The catching of minnows, for instance. . . .

I remember that once, when I was fishing for trout in a famous dry-fly river where they obstinately refused to rise, I came suddenly upon a very grave clerical gentleman who was so immensely concerned with the catching of minnows upon his fly-rod that he did not notice my approach. I stood 10 yards away, watching him, and when at last he saw me he smiled and said:

"Really, this is a very curious thing. There was a time when I could catch minnows on a fly as easy as winking. Now I've been at it half an hour and I haven't got one."

There was a big shoal of minnows close to the bank. The clerical gentleman dapped a very small black gnat at them, and drew it quickly through the water in front of their noses; a little swirl followed it, but the minnows were either too quick for him or too small for the hook. He was growing impatient and striking harder than was necessary; once his fly became caught in some thistles behind him.

"Damn!" he said unclerically, "and I did so want one, too!" He sounded petulant.

"Why do you want one so badly?" I asked.

He looked a little shy. "Well, you see, the trout *won't* rise, will they? And there's one down stream, under a willow-root. . . . Well, I'm *sure* he's a cannibal. He'd be better out of the water. If only I had a minnow—"

I grinned, and we suddenly became conspirators. It was sheer poaching, of course . . . but he was quite right, the trout wouldn't rise. . . .

"There's a way," I said, "with a worm. . . ." I was younger, you see, than he was, so perhaps I remembered more about minnows.

We grubbed about together in the mud on the bank, digging with the spikes of our fly-rods, and in the end we unearthed a huge and bilious-looking worm. It was about 6 inches long, I should think: a specimen worm. The clerical gentleman looked at it with diffidence and disfavour.

"If they won't take my fly," he said, "on an ooo hook, they won't get *that* inside them."

"That doesn't matter," I said, very wise about minnows. "They hang on to the worm and you flick them out over your shoulder, and pick them up among the grasses."

He caught his first minnow five minutes later, and put it in some water in the bottle which had contained his luncheon beer. When at last I left him, after a quarter of an hour, he had got nine, and was becoming fairly expert. I hope he caught his trout later, whether he poached it or not, for he deserved it; but when I turned round and had a last glimpse of him as I climbed over the stile he was still catching minnows, and I expect he forgot all about the cannibal under the willow-root and went on minnow-fishing till the light failed.

Plate XI

Angling is like that; it is not, for most of us, a matter of avoirdupois, and it is impossible to measure the delights of a day by means of the spring-balance. Certainly there are greedy and haughty ones among us, stern men who have their photographs taken beside heaps of monstrous fish, so that they look like fishmongers trying to sell their wares; or who dream constantly of glass-cases and taxidermists and the like; or who fish so seriously that they think one is blasphemous if one ventures a little joke by the waterside. . . .

Once I fished with such a man as these latter, on Slapton Ley in Devonshire, when a blazing sun had put the rudd off biting altogether. I grew tired of watching a motionless float, and towards evening I called to my friend and flippantly suggested that we should have a competition, the stake to be a pint of beer and the winner he who caught the greater number of little sprats, bleak and the like, in the space of half an hour—for these tiddlers were at least catchable. He regarded me sternly for a moment, and then damned me with a phrase.

"*Aquila non capit muscas,*" he said, for he was a scholar.

Luckily his sort is not very plentiful; and for the most part anglers are gentle and peaceable men, who fish not for the pot nor for the illustrated papers, but because they cannot help fishing. Did not old Izaak himself say that angling was "somewhat like poetry"? And who would think of measuring the quality of a poem by the number of its lines?

It is strange that there should be so strong an element of poetry in this business of rods and hooks and lines. Perhaps it is an echo of the water's music and the wild song which the dying rushes sing. Or perhaps it is there because angling is in a sense esoteric—there are mysteries about it, and where there is mystery mysticism is never far to seek. Again, there is no rhyme nor reason why one should angle; there is no firm logical basis upon which a man can stand and argue, "For this reason and for that do I go fishing." Indeed, the thing is very nearly a folly, and yet we anglers know in our hearts that it is very far from a folly indeed. Thus it is with poetry also—you have it or you have it not, and if you have it not, nothing in the world can make you understand it.

Again, there is mixed up with angling a certain flavour of strange adventure; and somehow—as with poetry—this is rather an adventure of the mind than of the body. It consists chiefly in the angler's saying to himself: "If I put my bait in that far eddy, if I cast my fly under that overhanging bush, none can say what may leap at it! It may, indeed, float down stream undisturbed; but, on the other hand, for all I know, the biggest fish in the river—nay, a bigger fish than has ever been caught here before—may lurk there ready to seize it. All I can *see* is a ripple of water, and a strong swirl, and the sun shining into green deeps; but nevertheless Leviathan himself—who can tell?—may lie there waiting among the weeds."

(Leviathan, of course, varies in size in different localities. In a good dry-fly river he is a 4-pounder; in a salmon river he weighs 50 pounds; but if you are fishing for dace this same Leviathan is just heavy enough to tip the spring balance over the 16 ounces; while to my parson friend who was so preoccupied with minnows, a 5-incher would have seemed a giant, an apparition, a whale!)

This element of adventure (which Dr. Van Dyke emphasised well when he said of angling that it was "tempting the Unknown with a hook") plays a great part, I am sure, in the fascination which the business exercises over us. We throw, not a die, but a feathered lure and we throw against thrilling chances! Skill and fortune are the twin gods who hold our rewards in their hands. Ovid, temporarily digressing from the discussion of another art—or sport?—pointed out:

"*Casus ubique valet: semper tibi pendeat hamus:*
Quo minime credis gurgite piscis erit"*—

lines which Mr. William Radcliffe chose as an inscription for his fishing diary, and which he translated into an English rhyming couplet thus:

"Chance everywhere counts much: *aye* work your hook:
Fish lurk in whirls where you'd least likely look."

Sound advice to all anglers in general and to salmon-fishers in particular!

Anglers, then, are a placid and humour-loving folk, content with their delight of the little things. They are poets and philosophers, adventurers and yet lovers of quietude and meditation. They (alone of sportsmen) unite almost ideally the *bios practicos* and the *bios theoreticos*. They are also masters of many moods. They know the secret of the little jokes which water makes as it hurries over the stones; they can laugh with the river, and sigh with the wind in the reeds.

Moreover, they have invented a new scale of values—or rediscovered an old one—for they have proved that the mighty salmon of Tweed or Dee is not necessarily more desirable and more eagerly to be sought than, in different circumstances, is the little leaping trout of Devonshire, nor even than a 5-inch minnow. (I have just thought that Smith Minor, the friend of Mr. Punch, if he should read this chapter by chance, will next term be construing *De Minimis* as "about minnows." My apologies to him if it leads him into trouble; but are not minnows the basis upon which all our angling is built up? Did we not catch them, and learn the joy of catching them, long before we heard of greenheart and split cane?)

* *Ars Amat.*, iii. 425-6.

And are they not as delightful in memory, those minnow-catching days so long ago, those expeditions after bleak and gudgeons and little perch, as those more recent hours of the mayfly and the cocked olive? For it is by the trifles that a day's angling is to be recalled, and not entirely by the number of fish and the weight of them. Long after you have forgotten that 2-pounder which you caught below the mill-wheel, you will remember—wistfully, if you are far away from it—how the water chuckled as it ran down under the sweeps.

And that reminds me of something else which I must quote and, if it be Rupert Brooke a second time, I cannot help it; for there are some things which leap to the pen's point as a trout leaps to a fly. It is a fragment from *Grantchester*:

> ". . . To smell the thrilling-sweet and rotten
> Unforgettable, unforgotten
> River smell, and hear the breeze
> Sobbing in the little trees.
> Say, do the elm-clumps greatly stand
> Still guardians of that holy land?
> The chestnuts shade, in reverend dream,
> The yet unacademic stream?
>
> . . . . . .
>
> Oh, is the water sweet and cool,
> Gentle and brown, above the pool?
> And laughs the immortal river still
> Under the mill, under the mill?"

He thought of his favourite stream thus as he sat, hot and miserable, in a Berlin café. How poignant those delights seemed to him then, how greatly to be desired! And yet of what trifles were they made up, the sleepy, serious chestnuts, the old, musty river-smell, the clumps of elms—what little things! And at the last, you will remember, to finish the whole poem, he asks eagerly:

> "Stands the Church clock at ten to three?
> And is there honey still for tea?"

There is a sort of splendid irrelevancy about those last two questions. In the same way, at some time when you are most worried and distressed, at some crisis in your life, when all your hopes are tottering and the thing that you have built subsides into chaos before your eyes, you will find yourself wondering, very likely: "Is the mayfly up yet on the little stream? Are they dancing up and down in the sunset, those little magical flies that look like fairies? And are the big trout flopping up at them, beneath the bushes, in the mill-pool, under the bridge?"

And then, very likely, you will remember many things suddenly—the meadow carpeted with cuckoo-flowers, which the country folk call milkmaids, and the way your waders would swish gently among them; the big rabbit-warren where Bint, the short-legged, tousled Sealyham lady, was lost for three hours one day last season (she nearly frightened the life out of you because you thought she was buried alive); the yellow-hammer with his "little-bit-o'-bread-an'-no-cheese," the chaffinch singing his roulade, the chiff-chaff in the elm tree, and the far cuckoo which is the sign and symbol of the English spring. You will see in memory the excited little skipper butterflies in the lane, and the frail orange-tips which poise so exquisitely on the umbels of the hedge-parsley; the steep bank where the water-rats hold their high-diving competitions, and pretend to be rising trout; the pollards which look like ghosts in the dusk; the crisp green buds on the hawthorns, which you used to call "bread-and-cheese"—and the hawthorn's milky flowers, with their dreamy smell; the dancing spinners, iridescent in sunlight, and the sailing duns which go to their fate so placidly with small wings bravely cocked to catch the soft day-breeze; the marsh marigolds in the wet places, and the laughing murmur of water, and the urgent whispering swish of the line; the molten glory of sunlight splashed on the stream between the willows, and the blue sky with its few clouds like sailing yachts; the sighing breeze that seems to come from nowhere late on a May afternoon, that whispers one secret to the rushes and suddenly dies, a messenger from Faerie, perhaps, with news for the Hamadryads . . . and then the final peace of sundown, which is like an epitaph upon the dead day.

So will you remember this little thing and that one, until your whole heart is aching with memories. Your fly-rod alone can help you, for it is a magic wand which can bring memories alive; and it will send you hurrying towards that field of lady's smock, and will show you in time how the spring can be a balm to cure sick souls. As for me, I can wish you no better thing than just such a river as Rupert Brooke describes, a river that laughs and makes you merry. I hope that it will smell just like that, and look just like that, and that there will be many fish in it; and that you will have good luck in the catching of them, with soft winds and friendly weather—and honey galore at the farm-house tea at your day's end!

THE END